ESSENTIAL TOOLS FOR MANAGEMENT CONSULTING

Professor Simon A. Burtonshaw-Gunn
is a practising management consultant with
significant experience in both the public
and private sectors covering a range of
organizations and industries. He has
undertaken assignments in Asia, North Africa,
the Middle and Far East, and Eastern Europe.
To support this experience he holds two Masters
degrees and a PhD in various strategic
management topics together with fellowship of
four professional bodies. This book follows the
popular *The Essential Management Toolbox*
(John Wiley & Sons, 2008).

Also available in this series

Essential Tools for Organizational Performance

Essential Tools for Operations Management

This is a must-have resource for all practising or aspiring management consultants.
Simon Burtonshaw-Gunn covers four key areas of consulting:

- The profession
- Developing consultancy
- Managing projects
- Delivery

The book also provides a top-ten of consultancy tools, with evaluations of their usefulness, strengths and weaknesses.

Featuring clear, jargon-free explanations and advice, and links and references to further resources for management consultants, this is a book you'll want to refer to over and over again.

ESSENTIAL
TOOLS FOR
MANAGEMENT
CONSULTING

Tools, Models and Approaches for Clients and Consultants

Simon A. Burtonshaw-Gunn

A John Wiley & Sons, Ltd., Publication

CONTENTS

ACKNOWLEDGEMENTS

From the feedback since the publication of my book *The Essential Management Toolbox* I have been asked to expand on the models and tools in a practical way; for me the value of the Toolbox book is to have a collection of tools which may be used for a variety of management assignments. Again in compiling this book I have to say that this would not have been possible without the fine efforts from all those management authors, research publications and course notes, etc. that I have collected over the years. As such I am greatly indebted to all whose work appears in the book, and also to my own teachers and mentors who have aided my own journey through many management topics.

I am very grateful to the publishers, individuals and copyright holders who gave their permission to allow previously published work to be used in this book and whilst every effort has been made to ascertain copyright and seek permission I apologize in advance for any omissions and would be pleased to correct these in any future edition.

Once again I am indebted to my friends at John Wiley and Sons for their support and encouragement. My sincere thanks also go to my friend, former colleague and regular academic writing partner, Dr Malik Salameh, for his significant input and support in this project, in providing constructive comments on my draft manuscripts and his willingness to pen a few words to set the scene for the reader.

FOREWORD

by Dr Malik Salameh

Once again Professor Simon Burtonshaw-Gunn has identified a significant area where his extensive consultancy expertise can provide an essential road map – all in one publication. In this book he addresses the most important aspects which any prospective management consultant or consultancy expert would need to consider in providing consultancy intervention and in turn satisfy both professional standards and corporate management expectations.

This is the second book in a series of sibling publications targeted at senior organizational decision makers, interim managers and consultancy practitioners, which should be utilized as a key enabler for accurately entering into the client and professional services arena in an informed, structured and rigorous manner. One of its key strengths is the fact that it emphasizes the level of up-front client relationship management effort and diagnostic investment necessary to ensure any consultancy commission is executed on a mutually beneficial basis.

Furthermore, it highlights the sheer variety of opportunities which currently exist within the business consulting profession and become available when consultancy output is fully aligned with client expectations and can be seen to embed true organizational value. This book continues to adopt a highly successful formula developed previously by the author of providing the user with comprehensive domain knowledge and then selecting a range of management tools and techniques which he believes are the most effective in consultancy delivery and in anticipating the real-world issues threatening an organization's performance.

Having professionally collaborated with the author in delivering international management consultancy in both public and private sectors, I believe this publication satisfies a hitherto untapped opportunity; that being to provide a unique publication which is easily accessible and strikes the careful balance of identifying consultancy as a career development opportunity, as a catalyst to improve business performance, and as a client organizational reference to aid delivery of optimal value when selecting consultants and engaging consultancy practices on either an internal or external basis, respectively.

The completeness and relevance of this publication extends beyond the expert practitioner, and demonstrates how consultancy tools and techniques may be deployed independently to address a particular client requirement or in a layered manner to provide a fully integrated and independent appraisal of the issues facing any business. I strongly recommend this book as an invaluable source of knowledge in supporting organizations and individuals to harness maximum benefit from consultancy relationships by cultivating the right operational ethos and utilizing robust methodologies to provide impartial analysis.

ABOUT THE AUTHOR

Professor Simon A. Burtonshaw-Gunn has over 30 years' working experience with a technical background in mechanical and nuclear engineering, research and development and on-site major plant commissioning followed by over 12 years in project management in both technical consultancy and hardware projects for the UK Ministry of Defence. He joined British Aerospace in 1994 (now BAE Systems) undertaking project management of specialist consultancy work within Russia, Ukraine and Belarus. He held the post of Head of Project Management before being appointed as a managing consultant leading a consultancy team undertaking assignments including business strategy planning, change management, organizational development and management training covering a range of organizations and industries. As a practising management consultant he has undertaken assignments in over 20 countries in Asia, North Africa, the Middle and Far East and Eastern Europe and currently is a principal management consultant for an international management consultancy company in the UK working in both the public and private sectors. To complement this experience he holds two Master's degrees and a PhD in various strategic management topics together with fellowship of four professional bodies including the Chartered Management Institute (FCMI) and the Institute of Business Consulting (FIBC).

He was a post-doctoral research fellow for four years at the Manchester Metropolitan University before relinquishing this at the beginning of 2005 to take up the role of a visiting professor at the University of Salford in Greater Manchester. Here he served for three years in the six-star research rated School of the Built Environment before being appointed as the first visiting professor to the Salford Business School in 2007. In addition, he held a two-year appointment as a member of the Court at the University of Leeds – itself a member of the Russell Group association of the top 20 UK research-intensive universities – until 2009.

Professor Burtonshaw-Gunn has been a research examiner for the UK's Chartered Institute of Purchasing and Supply (CIPS) since 2002 and is one of the founding members of an international academic research group (ISCRiM) with a focus on supply chain risk management. In connection with this group he has presented conference papers in Sweden, the USA, UK and Hungary together with a number of refereed publications, professional journal articles and chapters in four collaborative management textbooks. On the subject of risk management he has recently published a book covering "Risk and Financial Management in Construction" aimed at industry practitioners and post-graduate students. His popular book *The Essential Management Toolbox* covering management tools, models and notes aimed at students, managers and consultants was published by John Wiley and Sons in 2008.

INTRODUCTION

This book has been developed from an interest in the use of management tools and models published in January 2008 in *The Essential Management Toolbox: Tools, Models and Notes for Managers and Consultants*. This supplementary book describes a number of examples and shares the author's practical experience in the use of appropriate management tools and models taken from the Toolbox with a focus on identifying and describing the essential tools for those involved in undertaking management consultancy activities.

As an introduction this book comprises five broad and inter-related chapters commencing with an overview of the profession of management consultancy including the topics of added value, consultancy governance and ethics. Chapter 2 looks at the development of consultancy skills from both an individual and consultancy practice perspective. The management of consultancy projects is explored in Chapter 3 which suggests the use of a project management approach, the importance of understanding the assignment requirements and expectations, and adoption of risk management for consultancy projects. Chapter 4 describes the main consulting delivery approaches including problem solving, facilitation and communication. The final chapter covers the author's selected "Top-ten" consultancy tools and describes from practical experience how and where these tools are best suited to be used. Each of the topics of these five chapters has been chosen to provide a framework for both organizations and individuals to draw upon in the delivery of their consultancy services, as shown in Figure I.1.

The intent of writing this title has been to provide once again a suitable reference for aspiring, recently appointed or seasoned management consultants wishing to understand and undertake practical performance improvements relevant to their professional development

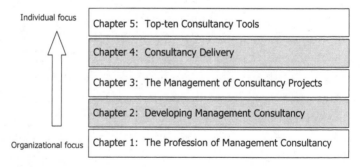

Figure I.1 Framework for management consultancy.

whether at the individual or organizational level and with an equal relevance to those employed as internal or external consultants within both the public and private sectors. The book describes a range of methodologies aimed to provide an underpinning knowledge of the practical tools that are open to consultants to employ on their assignments. In addition the opening chapter looks towards the profession itself in sharing some thoughts around added value and the issues of governance and ethical practice.

Whilst the intent has been to provide an opportunity to discuss some new models, the majority of the figures and models are taken from *The Essential Management Toolbox: Tools, Models and Notes for Managers and Consultants* published by John Wiley and Sons in 2008. Where the original source is not the author's, then the source is shown with each model discussed.

The book is designed as one of a series of sibling publications intended to group enabling management tools, techniques and models into related clusters giving consultancy practitioners a highly effective means of development at both an individual and practice level providing consultancy services. Other titles are *Essential Tools for Organizational Performance* and *Essential Tools for Operations Management*.

The structure follows the successful "Essential Management Toolbox" formula of integrating contemporary management tools, techniques and models with those developed from practical experience of addressing the challenges of management consulting across multiple industries. As with *The Essential Management Toolbox* and other books in this series full references are provided to guide the reader to where further information may be found. In addition each chapter is punctuated by key theme subheadings to aid navigation and provide a logical approach to each topic area.

CHAPTER 1

THE PROFESSION OF MANAGEMENT CONSULTANCY

INTRODUCTION

The aim of this first chapter is to set the scene by looking in general terms at: the consultancy profession and the types of consultants; the topic of added value applicable to both consultants and their clients; the role of governance in the profession; and finally to consider the importance of business ethics applicable to consultants and consultancy organizations.

DEVELOPMENTS IN MANAGEMENT CONSULTING

Management consultancy derives its revenues from clients in all areas of both public and private sectors. Whilst regarded as a large and diverse profession in terms of practising consultants and business turnover revenue, it is a volatile profession where individuals are mobile and practices are able to form and change rapidly. Unlike other professions, consultancy has little, if any, barriers to entry, and with an absence of any statutory regulation anyone is free to enter the workplace as a consultant irrespective of their level of experience, education or level of competence required for this profession. Indeed, this view is further complicated with free use of the title; from personal trainers to recruiters calling themselves consultants. Perhaps because of this there are two opposing opinions on management consultants; one often quoted view is that:

> Consultants are people who borrow your watch to tell you what time it is ... and then walk off with the watch.
> **From *Up the Organisation* by Robert Townsend**

The other view, happily, is about a symbiotic relationships and mutual reliance between "consultant" and "client".

The focus of this chapter is to better understand this professional service provision and the important and valuable role that management consultants can play in creating effective business cultures, in addition to sharing "best practice" and assisting in increased organizational performance. Indeed, if carefully selected, briefed and respected by their clients, management consultants can provide a valuable resource for organizations of all sizes, whether in the private, public or "not for profit" sectors.

Whilst there are a number of views on the role, scope and attributes of a management consultant ranging from "adviser to business" to "a specialist to bring about efficient management practices" the following list also captures for many individuals and businesses what management consultancy is about:

- The provision of information that may not be otherwise available to the client with the opportunity to gain an insight into current thinking in a particular industry or sector which can be benchmarked accordingly.
- The provision of specialist resources with skill sets to address a key problem or issue thoroughly which are either in short supply or non-existent within the client's organization. These may only be needed in the short-term and as such full-time recruitment to undertake this role would not be cost effective. In addition this may also offer opportunities to the client for the transfer of such skills to its own staff if commercially viable.
- The establishment of business contacts and linkages in order to assist in promoting the client's organization in new markets.

- The provision of expert opinions to enable line management to make decisions on what to do.
- Undertaking of diagnostic analysis with sophisticated tools not available to a client or their subordinates.
- Developing practical action plans based on "best-practice" and wider pan-industry experience.
- Improvement of systems and methods again with the ability to draw upon a wider knowledge base than resides within the client's organization.
- Training and development of management and staff to help them make more effective decisions relative to the business objective and long-term strategic direction.
- The provision of personal counselling, coaching, mentoring and training to support the development and retention of key knowledge workers.
- Implementation of difficult or unpopular decisions with responsibility for them; this may also include providing support to others through difficult situations.
- The ability to act as a messenger and carry information that is not moving up the organization by the normal communication route. This often includes easier access to senior managers and opportunities to provide independent or impartial advice.
- The ability to draw upon a wider range of established, tried and tested approaches as a basis of tailoring these for bespoke situations to suit client requirements.

- The ability to undertake work which requires objectivity and complete independence, for example, to gain acceptance to introducing a change that is unpalatable or difficult to achieve.
- The ability to take the pressure off the client by taking on the role of "scapegoat" for the introduction of new methods, systems and processes, etc.

For a more succinct view, the UK's professional body for consultancy (the Institute of Business Consulting) proposes the following definitions of the consultancy profession:

> Management consulting involves individuals, whether self-employed or employed, using their knowledge and experience, and their analytical and problem-solving skills, to add value into a wide variety of organisations within a framework of appropriate and relevant professional standards, disciplines and ethics.

In addition, the Institute of Business Consulting also offers the following definition of a management consultant:

> A management consultant is a person who is professionally engaged in advising on and providing a detached, external view of a company's management techniques and practices. A consultant can operate as a specialist or a generalist. The client's requirements dictate which skills and expertise are most appropriate and the situations in which to use a consultant.

Source: Institute of Business Consulting

From the opening comment about the profession being unregulated the Institute of Business Consulting itself is pursuing policies to set, maintain and raise the standards of both professionalism and competence for the profession. Leading on from the above definitions it is widely accepted that management consulting typically involves the identification and cross-fertilization of best practices, analytical techniques, change management, technology implementations, strategy development and coaching skills. However, such identification is merely a list of tools or competencies which the consultant may wish to draw upon in order to provide sound advice to business about efficient management practices. On this basis therefore one of the attributes of management consultancy can be considered to be the practice of assisting companies to improve their operational and hence financial performance through analysis of existing business problems together with the introduction of key performance metrics by which the organization can then be actively managed. The publication of the Geneva-based International Labour Organization (ILO) proposes that:

> Management consulting is an independent professional advisory service assisting managers and organizations in achieving organizational purposes and objectives by solving management and business problems, identifying and seizing new opportunities, enhancing learning and implementing changes.

The decision for an organization to use a firm of management consultants can arise due to a number of reasons; the first being that consultants can often provide an informed analysis by drawing upon their wider expertise and independent specialist skills than is available within the host organization. Second, it is often easier for an outsider to provide an objective appraisal by seeing the broader picture whilst realistically recognizing the organization's long-term requirements. This in itself may lead on to various outcomes such as change management, outsourcing, crisis management or detailed process consultation. The third reason arises where the use of a management consultant may be needed for the provision of additional temporary assistance to address an unexpected increase in the management workload, this can often arise in conjunction with the implementation of a major change programme or from a new development in management responsibility.

Having proposed these three reasons for the use of consultants it is clear that these can feature in the five broad generic consultancy purposes proposed by clients for their use of consultants irrespective of differences in the technical area of the intervention and in the specific intervention method used. According to the ILO these purposes are:

- Achieving organizational purposes and objectives.
- Solving management and business purposes.
- Identifying and seizing new opportunities.
- Enhancing learning.
- Implementing changes.

Consultancy advice, in the main, is provided from two areas – technical and behavioural – although of course there are many examples of where both skill sets are utilized on a single consultancy project. The technical dimension concerns the nature of management or business problems faced by the client organization and the way that this problem is analysed, recommendations offered and then resolved by the proposed implementation. Such technical management consulting usually draws upon knowledge of organizational structures, systems, processes, resource allocation and models of utilization to achieve efficient and effective business performance. The "human dimension" encompasses the interpersonal relationship in the client's organization, people's feelings about the problem, business environment, its current market position and the relationship between the consultant and the client as people. In this area the consultant's role is in providing advice to motivate, energize and empower people typically around organizational development, change management and human resource development. (Note: the topics of process management, change management and people-focused performance are discussed in detail together with supporting tools and models in *Essential Tools for Organizational Performance*.)

TYPES OF CONSULTANTS

Whilst the developments in management consulting above have started to identify the activities and different types of consultancy approaches, Edgar Schein suggested 40 years ago that consultancy provision could be divided into three principal categories which he termed: expert consulting, the doctor–patient model and process consulting. The selection of one of these categories is said to be as a result of the ownership of the problem and the authority vested in the most appropriate party to solve this. Figure 1.1 shows the two main strategies which are discussed below together with an alternative intermediate approach.

From Figure 1.1 "Expert" consulting is where the client seeks to purchase the provision of consultancy services by transferring ownership of the problem to the consultant. It is best used when the client has correctly diagnosed the problem and the consultant has the

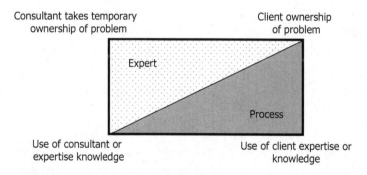

Figure 1.1   Consultancy approaches.
Figure adapted from text on pages 5 to 11 in Edgar F. Schien, *Process Consultation, its Role in Organizational Development.* Addison-Wesley, 2nd edition, 1988.

capability to provide the relevant competent expertise. This choice also requires the client to accept some risk in the advice and solution given as the problem may have been incorrectly thought through at the outset and the consultant may therefore have been asked to solve the "wrong" issue with the potential consequence of obtaining the wrong information or recommending an inappropriate solution.

At the other extreme is "Process" consulting which is often founded on the premise that the client owns the problem and continues to do so throughout the consultation process. In this approach the client accepts that the organization has problems but does not know what to do about them; as such the consultant is required to undertake a diagnosis as part of the intervention. Process consulting can be used to offer the client an understanding of the problem and identify the range of actions open for consideration. In the longer term the client will be capable of learning to embed these tools and techniques to help diagnose and solve their own organizational problems. It is then likely to understand the best approach to the implementation of the solution by linking this to its own business processes.

The compromise is a collaborative approach also referred to as the "doctor–patient" model which gives the consultant the task of diagnosing the problem and recommending what type of intervention will best provide a solution to the problem. This model is best employed when the diagnostic process is seen as being helpful to the client and information on the problem area will be provided in full and without exaggeration. The doctor–patient model can be used when the client will understand and correctly interpret the diagnosis provided by the consultant and will implement the prescribed solution resulting in long-term performance improvements after delivery of the intervention. Here the client will be responsible for the implication following the diagnosis and the continued momentum of the initiative.

Having looked at the three different types of consultant models there is also a distinction between internal and external consultancy interventions. An internal consultant already works inside part of the organization and is tasked with helping other parts of the same business; in the main, the use of internal consultants is becoming increasingly common in large organizations where they have both the financial resources to afford such full-time assistance and where they have sufficient work, or indeed problems, to keep them gainfully employed. In many cases internal consultancy develops from the use of business improvement teams often formed to solve an immediate problem which go on to address short- and longer-term business needs, introduction of new legislation, sudden changes in market dynamics and/or fiscal pressures. These share a number of features with externally consultants, such as their abilities to:

- fix or install something;
- introduce a new product or service;

- solve a problem;
- undertake research of the feasibility of a certain change;
- re-engineer or reorganize a process; or lastly
- create a new function based on a clear vision with the motivation and support to make it happen.

Internal consultants may also be used to commission external consultants; to brief them about the culture and context of the assignment; to ensure that they are compliant with the governance requirements of the business; and to assess if they provide value for money.

The different types of consultant are shown in Figure 1.2 where the consulting activity can take either an advisory or an executive role, and is undertaken by external or by an organization's own in-house consultants.

Figure 1.2   Types of consultant.
From *Managerial Consulting – A Practical Guide*, 2nd edition. C.J. Margerison, 2001. Reproduced with permission of Gower Publishing.

Examples of internal consultancy areas of work may include IT, finance and increasingly HRM where they may be involved in performance improvement or implementing change programmes. Whilst some may operate at a strategic level, this is a real exception as at this level the senior management prefers paying for the external perspective, a service not so readily provided by internal consultants. This also offers the board a level of privacy and comfort as an external mentor or advisor can be seen as a "critical friend". It is noted that at this level credibility, status, internal politics, legacy issues and reputation are the main challenges facing internal consultants and it is clear that internal and external consultants wield different amounts of power and senior level influence.

Role A is the conventional notion of an external consultant who provides specialist advice on contract for a time to clients.

Role B has its origin in the construction and IT industries particularly where a project manager from an outside organization has responsibility for delivering an assignment but acts as a consultant to the clients and as a line manager in their own organization.

Role C has a full-time executive to act as a consultant to colleagues in a coaching and supporting way.

Role D employs internal consultants for their specialist advice such as health and safety, finance, marketing, legal, etc.

Naturally, there are advantages and disadvantages in using internal consultants, and whilst the most obvious benefit is that they inevitably cost much less that external consultants this perception cannot be treated in isolation as further consideration will recognize that internal consultants also have other costs not immediately considered when making such a statement, for example the cost of holidays, sickness leave, training, pension and health care provisions and the cost of any unproductive time. Whilst in the same debate external consultants may cost more initially for the work, there is no obligation from the client with respect to the same additional costs of holidays, training, etc. This is not to say that external consultants should be used in preference to internal resources or indeed vice versa as both will have attributes which they are able to bring to the assignment undertaking. As shown in Figure 1.3 there are a number of reasons for

Reasons for using internal consultants on market research	Reasons for not using internal consultants on market research
They are flexible and can undertake the consultancy work in conjunction with other activities.	Can be under-resourced as they may be perceived as a cost.
They offer value for money in that they can be used as and when required.	May be overused – and given too much work because they are seen to be "free" and therefore always available for use.
They are often very knowledgeable about the company and its culture and can understand the difficulties that it faces to a greater extent than external resources.	May have incomplete range of skills required in order to undertake specific needs.
They need to be fully briefed to allow them to use their own experience to interpret the objectives of the task and use this knowledge to modify the questions if necessary in order to obtain the required information.	They need to be fully briefed and know the broader reasons for collecting the data. Without such information they are likely to ask the wrong questions in the survey and the results will not meet the objectives of the task.

Figure 1.3 Considerations on the use of internal consultants.

and against the use of internal consultants when considering, as an example, undertaking market research.

Having mentioned above the different costs of internal and external consultants it is common practice for departments to have an allocated number of internal consultancy days which they may call upon when required. Whilst the current economic climate may see an increase in the use of internal consultants there is often a view of "not valuing what you don't pay for" – a common problem with respect to the credibility of internal consultants. A good use of both is to have external consultants review an internal consultant team's work or, at least, provide their views on the same problem and hence they can be seen to validate the internal approach and act as a barometer for aligning both outputs. Although external consultants are able to draw upon their depth and breadth of experience it is often at a premium cost and there is always the pressure to end the arrangement as soon as practicable. On the other hand, internal consultants are employees who will see the project through to completion and have a vested interest in its success.

Having looked at individual consultants it is also clear that consultancy firms can themselves be categorized into a number of specialist areas such as:

- **Generalist**, these are the larger firms offering a wide range of services from strategy consulting and human resources through to IT and outsourcing on a global basis. Many of these firms grew out of financial services or IT companies.

- **Strategy consultants** offering strategic advice to companies on a project-by-project basis.
- **Human resource consultants** offering specialist HR advice.
- **Information technology consultancy firms**, which offer specialist IT advice such as defining information needs, systems analysis and design, and making hardware evaluations.
- **Financial consultants** offering specialist advice including the installation of budgetary control systems, profit planning and capital and revenue budgeting.
- **Niche firms**, these are a result of consultants leaving the larger firms and setting up their own consultancy firms in a particular sector or offering unique specialist advice.

Having identified some of the purposes around the use of consultancy and the different practitioner types and attributes, the focus of this chapter now looks at exploring the mutual benefits of the use of management consultants by discussing the concept of added value where the term "added value" refers to that which exists beyond the payment of fees to the consultant, or the receipt of advice and assistance to the client.

CONSULTANCY ADDED VALUE

The Value Chain model developed by Professor Michael Porter can be of benefit to companies in examining their overall performance and support industry-wide bench-marking; it does not, however, seem easily applicable for companies wishing to identify their added value when delivering technical or management consultancy services. Indeed in looking at the world of consultancy it is suggested that as the contractual relationship between the supplier (consultant) and the buyer (client) is satisfied by the exchange of knowledge, assistance, advice and so on, in return for agreed fees, that this arrangement does not at first sight support the concept of added value. Having said this, it is proposed that the relationship does indeed offer a number of opportunities where both parties are able to benefit over and above the contracted value of the services provided and hence the use of the term added value can then be wholly justifiable. The often quoted adage that:

> Give a man a fish and you feed him for a day. Teach him how to fish and you feed him for a lifetime.
> **(attributed to Tao philosopher, Lao Tzu 570–490 BC)**

is a perfect example of consultancy added value. In today's consultancy business, added value can be seen in a number of ways including knowledge transfer and training – both contemporary adoptions of Lao Tzu's philosophy.

Examples of added value for both the consultant and the client organizations suggested in Figure 1.4 are described in the following two lists:

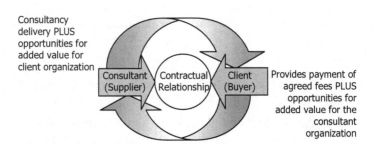

Figure 1.4 Consultant/client relationship and expectations. From *Extending the Concept of "Added-Value" to Consultancy*. Professional Consulting, Institute of Management Consultants, UK. S.A. Burtonshaw-Gunn, 2005.

List 1: Examples of added value to consultants

- **Business development (new work):** Opportunities to use the consultancy tasks as a natural way for follow-on work as part of a "one-stop-shop" approach where knowledge of the project and client organization will already be known to the consultancy provider.

- **Business development (extension of work):** Developing further work by utilizing advanced knowledge of client needs, experience of client's culture and hence the ability to offer a vastly reduced "learning curve".

- **Business development (new clients):** With overseas projects there may also be the potential to develop work in the same geographic region based on new, and current, local knowledge.

- **Project management:** Using a consultant's own network and established supply chain to undertake work or gain support from other specialist consultants.
- **Consultancy track record:** Establishing a track record with a client in an industry or work type which can then be used to market services to other potential clients in adjacent industries or markets. Such experience can be marketed with a multiplier affect on the consultancy's impact on the client's overall business performance.
- **Client knowledge:** Developing knowledge of clients and other businesses as part of ongoing consultancy practice enhancement.

List 2: Examples of added value to clients

- **Speed and cost:** Provision of rapid response and flexible resourcing from the supplier (consultant) with immediate use of required skills and experience to undertake the client's task. This also means savings on recruitment, training and termination costs if this is not to be a whole time resource.
- **Specialist advice:** Acquisition of advice on processes, etc. into the client's business as "best practice" examples drawn from wider consultancy assignments and other industry experience.
- **Additional resourcing:** Consultant introduction of other specialist consultants which can be used to support the client's project requirements without

delays in further tendering, assessment and selection by client.

- **Project risk reduction:** The benefit of using a specialist consultant is in gaining expert advice and the opportunity for the client to reduce any risk contingency allocation based on such knowledge and experience.
- **Value more than cost:** Clients can value consultancy delivery with a multiplier affect with respect to the impact on the business, for example decisions made and processes introduced have impact on the success of its larger-scale business operations, for example a one-off £5000 fee for consultancy work may save the business £50 000 per annum.
- **Knowledge transfer and training:** The client's staff can learn from consultants either informally, as part of a collaborative team or by shadowing – a modern-day version of the earlier Lao Tzu quotation.

Another example of added value equally applicable to both consultant and client organizations occurs from collaborative working where such joint understanding offers added value to the project and its participants through improved working practices, joint decision making and problem resolution, and a reduction, or even elimination, of financial claims for extras or disruptive working between the two parties. A full chapter covering performance and collaborative working is provided in

Essential Tools for Organizational Performance published by John Wiley and Sons.

BIG-PICTURE "ADDED VALUE" FOR CONSULTANTS

Within a consultancy organization it is proposed that the concept of added value be examined at either one of three main time-related opportunities. The first opportunity is at the pre-contract stage where a subjective assessment can be made regarding the added value to the practice for undertaking a certain piece of consultancy work in relation to its future strategic aspirations. Such considerations at this stage will include the fit with the overall company in terms of market development, particularly if this represents a venture into a new target country or region. Although subjective this can be represented by the following equation:

Value added = The anticipated consultancy fee multiplied by the value of strategic fit (a value between 0 to 1) less the cost to bid and win the consultancy work

Whilst this approach may be useful it is accepted that there are some difficulties with the above proposed equation as the total revenue for the consultancy work may not be known at the outset making the total fee income difficult to calculate with absolute confidence. The weighting of the work for the consultancy practice is added to demonstrate how it undertakes work in line with its own business objectives and long-term development ambitions – rather than just taking on work as a source of income.

The second opportunity to examine the value added of consultancy work arises at the project execution stage where a much more quantitative analysis can be undertaken. This can cover the **cost** of the consultancy in relation to the **value** of the project and the effectiveness of the services provided in supporting the project's time, cost and quality requirement; the impact of the advice provided to minimize business risk or provide improvements from the introduction of any new processes and practices.

Value added = Value of the overall project multiplied by the strategic value to business less the value of the consultancy contract

Identifying this level of added value can be used by the consultancy practice in its promotion and marketing activities, especially where supported by client testimonials.

Before discussing the final assessment phase it is worth returning to consider Lao Tzu's fishing example as it is often difficult to establish with any degree of accuracy the long-term value of consultancy actions and over what timescales these can be attributed. The value added assessment at the project completion stage focuses on capitalizing the experience of the consultancy work completed by either a subsequent award for work with the same client or alternately securing work with a new client based upon this initial experience. Again this is expressed in the proposed formula shown below, which also reflects the erosion of value added as a function of time.

Value added = Consultancy fee multiplied by the value of new work for same client (or multiplied by the value of new work in the same geographic area or similar work with a new client); this value is then divided by time in years

The subtlety of this formula is its ability to recognize that the learning and benefits from completed projects have a natural "half-life" such that the value of recent projects is much more relevant to winning new work than those completed say five or so years ago.

Within the above three opportunities is the fundamental importance of the relationship between the consultancy assignment and the organization's business objectives which may be operationalized through its chosen marketing strategy, see also Chapter 2. In addition to this is the relationship between the consultancy requirement and that of its staff capabilities and their development needs.

THE ROLE OF GOVERNANCE
IN CONSULTANCY

Whilst there are practice guidelines and standards applicable for the delivery of professional services including the Institute of Business Consulting's own "Code of Professional Conduct", this area is now examined to see how both consultancy organizations and individual consultants recognize that they each have responsibilities during the execution of management consultancy assignments. Both the company's and individual's consultancy delivery activities should be undertaken within an organizational governance framework and the conduct of the consultant must reflect professional ethical responsibility. This is by no means a new concept, indeed one of the first Codes of Professional Practice was the oath believed to be written by Hippocrates in the 4th century BC and although taken by physicians to cover ethical practice by the requirement to "abstain from whatever is deleterious and mischievous" it is suggested that this philosophy is applicable to today's business undertakings as it has been to the medical profession for almost two and a half thousand years.

The widely held view of "governance" is that of a suite of discrete management processes belonging to the senior management of the business which provides a framework, guidelines and self-imposed rules for business decision making which defines expectations, grants power and can be used to verify performance.

Another common definition is that governance is the capability to set and evaluate performance against objectives; authorize a strategy to achieve objectives while addressing risks; and stay within legally mandated and voluntary boundaries. The term "governance" itself has the same roots as the word "government" and is derived from the Greek term cybernetics (kybernētēs) where its definition is:

> the study of feedback and derived concepts such as communication and control in living organisms, machines and organizations.
>
> **Source:** *Oxford English Dictionary*

Whilst there is widespread general acceptance that it is fundamental to long-term business performance that work is conducted in a professional way, it is proposed that there is a natural link between the guiding processes of governance and that of ethics; a topic also covered in this chapter and eloquently summed up by Achal Raghavan's (2006) article commenting on ethics and governance in India:

> Good ethics and governance are not just "moral" or "compliance" issues. In the long term, they are essential behavioural traits for the organization that strengthen brand equity and help ensure stable growth.

Key from this quotation is the importance that many companies will place on helping to achieve long-term growth. In business, such governance may be regarded as

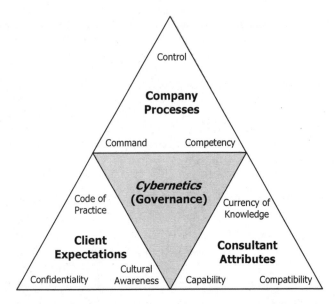

Figure 1.5 The trilateral "C" model of consultancy governance.

the action of developing and managing consistent, cohesive policies, processes and the provision of decision rights for a given area of responsibility. In a practical sense for consulting businesses this can be achieved through addressing the following trilateral issues shown in the author's model of Figure 1.5 and discussed below. This model can be used to provide a robust framework to address the topic of governance for a consultancy practice.

First, in heavy type are shown three primary governance areas for consultancy practices to consider; these being Company processes, Client expectations and Consultant attributes. Each of these primary topics is supported by a lower level of three further areas.

In looking at organizational governance are the **Company processes,** the model shows three inter-related management functions, these being:

- **Command:** This should address how the consultancy activities are effectively managed through a systematic and clear delegated authority process and adherence to company consultancy processes. This element will have to consider and include delegation of the authority to develop, review and amend such processes.
- **Control:** This should describe how the consultancy business and projects are audited to ensure adherence to relevant processes.
- **Compatibility:** This will need to describe how the match between individual consultants to the client is assessed in terms of their technical/business skills and relevant experience to undertake the client's works.

Next to be considered are the **Consultant's attributes** which are comprised of a further three inter-related factors which may contribute to the organization's governance from a peer group or self-assessed input:

- **Capability:** This should describe how the company supports the consultancy skills and experience and how they are maintained and further developed.
- **Competency:** This describes the maturity of an individual's knowledge, skills and track record which may be used in the provision of advice or actions with particular reference to safety, health, environ-

ment, legislation requirements, business practices and so on.

- **Currency of knowledge:** This should explain the onus on the consultancy practice to ensure that their consultant's knowledge is kept up to date and linked to cutting-edge developments in their domain field.

The final set of three factors represents the **Client's expectations** which may also be considered to contribute to the formal governance of the consultancy organization; these are shown in the model as being:

- **Cultural awareness:** This should cover how the individual consultant is matched to the client in terms of understanding and empathy of political, religious, historical and social influences.
- **Code of practice:** This covers how the individual consultants required behaviour traits are articulated and embraced and are evident to the client.
- **Confidentiality:** This should describe how the consultancy practice and individual consultant deals with client confidentiality, data protection and intellectual property rights (IPR).

It is interesting to note that it is the final part of the model which brings to the fore the factors which the profession would immediately have in its mind with respect to this topic: those of commercial confidentiality and an almost unwritten expectation that engaged consultants would operate in line with a code of conduct. Indeed, such a code of practice is often regarded as the basis of ethical behaviour and responsibility and naturally leads to the discussion on ethics in consultancy.

ETHICS AND CONSULTANCY

In recent years the perceived lack of individual ethical behaviour has received increasing publicity and scrutiny in the media. The public response has been an increased level of expectations of higher standards from public servants, elected representatives and professional advisors. Whilst the philosophical subject of "ethics" as a whole covers a range of subtopics one of these is business ethics which examines rules and principles within a commercial context, the various moral or ethical problems that can arise in a business setting, and any special duties or obligations that apply to persons who are engaged in commerce.

Clearly, from this understanding it should be stressed that ethical responsibility is a necessary feature of all business life in the way that organizations conduct their business operations whether commercially focused or in the not-for-profit arena; indeed, this is perhaps more acute for charitable organizations funded by public and/or private donations. Typically, such issues are usually addressed by cascading to all employees a corporate ethics code, although imposition can so often upset some staff who believe that they are professional enough not to be given the company's rules on how to behave especially where there is a lack of respect for the senior leadership team.

In focusing on the consultancy profession, many consultants will undertake their work through adherence to their consultancy practice's quality and professional processes in terms of a providing a traceable audit route with verification of their methodology used, conclusions drawn and recommendations or actions proposed to the client; however, the ethical aspect is often less overtly regulated, relying almost exclusively on an individual's personal *modus operandi*. Perhaps because consultants often have access to information and knowledge from a range of client organizations the way that they treat such privileged information needs to be managed from a confidential and ethical standpoint as breaking such trust will naturally result in detrimental and potential legal consequences for both the individual client and the wider consultancy practice. This relationship with the client suggests the need to conduct consultancy business against key criteria such as accountability, honesty, integrity, openness and respect. Putting these professional requirements into practice is widely undertaken and is "second nature" to many of those who have gained a level of consultancy experience; for newcomers to the profession these attributes often need to be checked by peer review and mentoring as part of their professional development plans.

In comparing a number of example codes of practice, many professional bodies issue these to assist their membership and on examination they largely share a similar theme of encouraging the consultant to act professionally, in good faith and to the highest standards for the work objectives. In addition, there are two further topics within this subject, namely transparency and vulnerability; transparency covers the degree to which there is openness in the situation, such as how much knowledge or information has been made available to the client. If there is not a full and complete level of openness, the reason for such lack of transparency will need to be carefully examined by the consultant. The second term of "vulnerability" refers to the level to which each of the client's interests may be at risk as a result of the proposed consultancy action (or indeed inaction). Clearly, both of these need to be properly managed and for this reason consultants should carry an appropriate level of professional indemnity insurance.

Furthermore, wherever possible consultants are expected to react positively to the client's needs and respond to their feedback as part of the well-known and widely used "Plan-Do-Act-Review" quality cycle model. In addition to these requirements, certain legislative instruments will need to be observed. Typically, these will cover discrimination (in all its guises), employment, health and safety and any specific industry relevant legislation or accepted industry standards. On the "softer" side are expectations on ethics around integrity, misrepresentation and openness. The UK-based association "Professional Contractors Group" offers ethical practice advice to their members covering the above in addition to advisory notes on client education, competence, confidentiality and intellectual property rights (IPR) including programme and software considerations. In looking wider at consultancy assignments in a business context, the Institute of Business Ethics proposed that any resulting business decision should follow a simple three stage test:

- First, in questioning the perception of transparency and openness, does the client organization mind others knowing what it has decided?
- Second, what is the effect of the decision and who does the decision affect or hurt?
- Third, is the topic of fairness by questioning if the decision will be considered fair by those affected?

Finally, whilst every consultancy organization is free to develop its own corporate code of professional practice those with overseas business contracts may benefit from the lessons cited by the International Business Ethics Institute (IBEI) on mistakes that organizations make in developing a single global ethics programme. The IBEI suggests that these mistakes include:

- Not integrating international personnel into the development process.
- Discounting the importance of promoting the program as a competitive advantage.
- Basing company policies on legal requirements in their home domestic market.

- Appointing headquarters staff or expatriates to fill ethics positions.
- Offering training materials only in their home language.
- Using the word "ethics" extensively in program materials.
- Focusing on the few cultural differences rather than acknowledging the many cultural similarities.

Source: International Business Ethics Institute

It is suggested that the above IBEI list is based on practical international experience and that even large organizations may benefit from such ethics advice. A closing point on this subject is the difference between independent consultants and those allied to a particular product or software programme from either the consultant's own company or one if its partners. Whilst providing impartial advice is easy for the first group; it may be less so for the second if they are also tasked with generating additional client income from allied product sales. It is suggested, therefore, that clients also need to be aware at the outset of such pressures or agendas when selecting consultants with an expectation of receiving unbiased and independent business advice. On this note clients should look to membership of appropriate professional bodies, evidence of professional indemnity cover and the prevalence of their qualifications as being an important part of their consultant selection process.

CHAPTER 2

DEVELOPING MANAGEMENT CONSULTANCY

INTRODUCTION

This second chapter commences by exploring both the individual and consultancy practice's development and then looks at its approach to marketing its services. It next discusses the important consultancy tool of networking and finally examines the value of understanding the client's requirements as the first step in developing the relationship and the process leading to the award of a contract.

INDIVIDUAL DEVELOPMENT

Without exception, and not unreasonably, clients expect consultants to be "professional" however rarely do they understand that consultancy *per se* is unregulated with no barriers to entry and where anyone can set themselves up to practise as a management consultant. In fact qualifications in any business or management field which may be used to demonstrate a level of business understanding, knowledge and skills are not needed to undertake fee-earning work, as a common approach is for consultants to secure work purely on the basis of their technical qualifications and domain knowledge. Large practice consultancy organizations have their own methodologies which they religiously instill into their consultants as a way of achieving a level of quality assurance; as a way to be consistent in their approach, programme and outputs; and as a way to have some comfort from a governance aspect as their approach has been tried and tested in a number of situations. This training, common within the large "Tier 1" consultancy practices, fits well into the development of individual professional consultants and as part of a wider organizational competency management process, where the elements may be considered to be:

- **Competencies** – How they go about their work.
- **Attitude** – How they prepare for work.
- **Skills** – What they can do.
- **Knowledge** – What they know.
- **Differentiation** – What unique benefits they bring.

Over the last decade there has been a proliferation of smaller consulting organizations and it is these smaller organizations – down to self-employed, one-man consultancy businesses and internal consultancy groups – who are often unable to commit time and funds to such development and usually rely more on their experience than any formal learning and development. However, the proficiency of the above four areas will contribute to the professionalism of management consulting and are applicable to a number of activities required for consultancy delivery such as communications, teamworking, innovation, facilitation and problem solving to name but a few. In looking wider at the requirement for professionalism within consulting it is proposed that the following eight features are necessary:

- Competency, attitude, skills and knowledge (as shown above).
- A commitment to be cognisant of advances in the profession and their domain knowledge area in order to provide a currency of information and best practice knowledge.
- The concept of service and wider social interest.

- Professional approach with adherence to ethics and standards.
- Self-discipline and self-control.
- Trust and confidentiality.
- Impartiality and objectivity.
- Flexibility, quality and "value for money".

It is suggested then that the development of competencies, attitudes, skills and knowledge is linked into the individual's performance as shown in Figure 2.1, itself part of a performance management system, described in more detail in the sister publication *Essential Tools for Organizational Performance*.

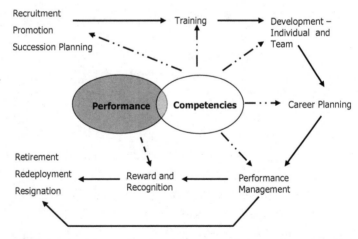

Figure 2.1 The cycle of recruitment, training and career management as part of a performance management system.
From *The Essential Management Toolbox: Tools, Models and Notes for Managers and Consultants*. S.A. Burtonshaw-Gunn, 2008.

Whilst this figure suggests a close working relationship between HR and functional managers as part of a cyclical business process, investment in the training and development aspects of the model should be undertaken as part of a wider programme of management consultancy competency with objectives around the four areas of competencies, skills, attitude and knowledge.

The only professional institution in the UK representing management consultants is the Institute of Business Consulting (IBC) which has its own competency model that can be used by individuals and practices to determine their future training and development requirements against a competency matrix covering three levels termed "development", "independence" and "mastery". Many large consultancy practices often have their own competency requirements allied to career progression which typically range across more levels from researcher, analyst, junior consultant, consultant, managing consultant up to partner level. The advantage of IBC's competency profile tool is that it allows for a clear recognition of individual skills between job transfers whether inside the same company or externally to a new consultancy company. With no tangible product it is the competency, knowledge, standing and gravitas of the consultant that very often provides a consulting practice with not just fee income but added value from the ability to use this for the benefit of the company in future business development. The IBC Management Consultancy Competence Framework is well established and its origins can be traced to its previous organization, the Institute of

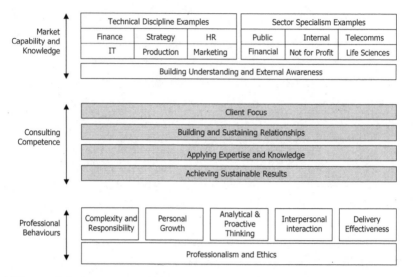

Figure 2.2   Management Consultancy Competence Framework.
Reproduced with kind permission of the Institute of Business Consulting.

Management Consultancy. The model shown in Figure 2.2 is taken from the 2002 document on the Competence Framework and although is the same in format, logic and requirements, this model is not illustrated in the latest version of the Framework document.

The professional behaviours such as governance and ethics have been discussed in Chapter 1; within this model all the elements relate to the individual consultant. Although the large consulting organizations provide training for their staff which results in a uniform approach to problem solving and consultancy assignments it has to be recognized that both the smaller consultancy and indeed internal consultancy groups are not as wedded to a set tool or methodology and as such may offer a broader range of solutions than just those in large practice vogue or which are more convenient for the consultancy provider.

If consultancy is a new activity for an organization then training and other development activities should be regarded as being very important. Even with the most qualified, experienced and professional consultants, organizations still need to attract new clients and retain their existing ones; as such marketing of the consultancy's up-to-date knowledge should be regarded as part of their marketing message and a key facet of their intellectual capital asset and talent management strategy.

MARKETING CONSULTANCY

It has to be said that marketing a consultancy service where there is often no actual product, where the consultant needs to understand the issues of the potential client base, and where the marketplace is potentially huge, requires a systemic, or at least a considered and targeted approach. Whilst it is easy to produce a brochure and mail it out in a confetti fashion, this clearly is not the ideal approach; and certainly one that is least likely to connect with the intended decision makers of the target client audience. A point to be returned to later.

An ideal starting point is to understand the consultant team's offering and how this may be matched to market needs. As such, agreeing a consultancy practice vision and mission statement is a useful exercise as this can focus the team into developing a mutually agreed marketing plan. However, it has to be said that this is not absolutely necessary as it is possible just to make it up as you go along, although such an unplanned approach makes monitoring progress difficult in the absence of a "route map" for comparison.

In planning to market a consultancy offering, the skills, knowledge and experience, i.e. the competencies of the staff, need to be articulated to show what type of work the consultancy will do and perhaps what it might do in the future. Figure 2.3 shows how having a shared vision may be used to expand the development of the consultancy services by prompting consideration of markets, resources, competencies, competitors and so on. It can then be used to set short-term and medium-term objectives for converting the goals into reality by assigning actions. These should be detailed in its marketing plan.

Having produced a marketing plan based on the above analysis the next stage is to put this into operation. In trying to raise the profile of the consultancy team this may be done in a passive way, for example production of articles, seminar presentations, blog and website usage, etc.; alternatively, this may take a more proactive approach by placing adverts in client targeted publications and

Figure 2.3 Consultancy marketing considerations.

direct mail, brochure, poster campaigns and so on. The prime objective is to connect with the potential client in a way that a meeting to discuss the client's issue and the consultancy's offering becomes a natural and easily arranged event. Connor and Davidson (1997) propose that there are six client-centred marketing activities that when incorporated into a marketing plan will provide a competitive advantage, these are:

- Selecting a targeted industry-market niche for special attention.
- Market research to develop an insider's understanding of the industry and markets.

- Building a favourable awareness and earning an insider's reputation with targeted members of the niche.
- Preparing, positioning, promoting and providing added value solution to their needs.
- Building strong, value-based relationships with all who are or can be influential to your marketing goals.
- Leveraging your knowledge, skills, experience and resources.

In support of the above methodology to target potential selected clients, rather than adopting an untargeted mailing approach, Leach and Moon in their book *Pitch Perfect* offer the following matrix model (shown as Figure 2.4) which may be used to plan how best to approach the identified clients.

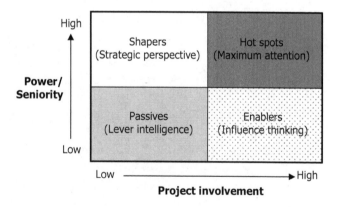

Figure 2.4   Pressure points matrix.
From *Pitch Perfect* by J. Leach and J. Moon. Capstone Publishing Ltd, 2003.

From the model in Figure 2.4 the position of the individuals in the target client organizations may be mapped on the matrix to determine how they may be approached. This is detailed below:

- **Hot spots** are individuals that hold budget responsibility and should be of prime importance to business developers as they often carry the maximum weight in the decision-making process. Personal credibility is at stake with these "hot spots" and as such the consultant will only have one chance to impress them.
- **Shapers** are often the most senior individuals within an organization concerned with strategy and direction. These would typically be individuals whose day-to-day role would not involve them in a project as they tend to take a more strategic perspective on purchasing decisions and would ensure that the decision is in the interests of the overall strategy, policy and direction of the business.
- **Enablers** are project individuals who have a day-to-day high degree of involvement with projects and are often part of the decision-making team.
- **Passives** are the supporting personnel, most likely at the administrative level involved in projects. It should be noted that these often appear to be more influential than they really are; however, they can be very beneficial in finding out company intelligence. They are usually more accessible and can be used to impart knowledge on key decision makers, policy, strategies, personalities and needs.

The importance of the matrix is its use for plotting current contacts in both existing and potential clients, these can be colour coded (red, amber and green, for example) to show the strength of the relationship which can indicate strengths and weaknesses and where to direct attention in developing the consultancy relationship further.

Tool 5 in Chapter 5 covers the elements of marketing in the match between the seller's approach to price, place, product and promotion and the market's reaction in terms of matching customer, cost convenience and communication. Whilst this tool may be useful to consultants in undertaking work for a client it can of course also be used when considering the marketing of the consultant's professional services. Additional marketing models are provided in the sister book *Essential Tools for Operations Management*.

DEVELOPING CONSULTANCY THROUGH NETWORKING

The wider topic of networking is discussed in the publication *Essential Tools for Organizational Performance* as part of its relationship with Knowledge Management. In this chapter the focus is on the use of personal networking that management consultants may undertake as part of their marketing activities. Here networking is concerned with relationships between people and can cover ways in which people make or are helped to make professional contacts with each other and how to make the most of such relationships.

Considering how much time is actually available to individuals to "network", to meet new people and explore common interests, etc. when faced with other demands upon available time, then the selection of where, when and how often to network should be regarded as a serious decision. On the basis of available time it is then possible to select which networking groups or events to target and attend; these can cover any one of the three types of professional networking groups which offer different benefits:

- Some groups provide opportunities to interact with prospective employers and clients, e.g. "business link" breakfast meetings where smaller businesses are encouraged to share experiences and ideas to improve in-house knowledge.
- Some groups enable their members to keep abreast of the latest developments, such as technical products or managerial processes. These are typical of many professional institutes' local branch meetings and special interest groups such as the Chartered Management Institute's Women in Management, Police and Care Management groups.
- Some groups provide opportunities for career skills development that will enable attendees to learn more about self-marketing, interviewing and making

a successful transition, an example of this is alumni associations.

In addition to these professional networking groups is the use of a more informal casual network such as family and friends, local school PTAs and friends of arts or charity groups as shown as Group 4 in Figure 2.5.

Having identified outward facing external networking it should be noted that there are also internal networks typically formed through proximity and organizational structure rather than by invitation. The purpose of the Group 5 internal networks of Figure 2.5 should be to allow an individual to develop their potential and for them in turn to contribute to the development of others through knowledge sharing. This internal network can also be used to share information about each other's

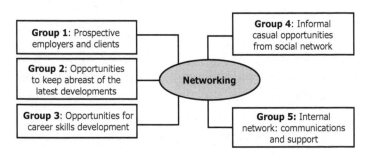

Figure 2.5 Networking groups.
From "Networking – a personal view" by S.A. Burtonshaw-Gunn. Published in *Professional Consulting*, Issue 20, 2007. Reproduction with permission.

skills and experience rather than just using the knowledge for which an individual was engaged.

Whilst many people profess to have access to a large network, for the vast majority of these this is passive and often outdated and rarely used to any tangible benefit. It is therefore suggested that it is often much more effective to be active in one professional association where people get to know who you are and what you do, and are able to trust you as a colleague or member rather than as a stranger. Furthermore involvement through a network's committee or organizing team will provide opportunities to get you involved in activities that in turn will enable greater interaction with others and foster a strong personal network. Whilst there is a practical restriction on the amount of people anyone can know, the interaction with groups offers a linkage to others through the use of a network. Indeed, as each network node is connected to another network through people, the book *The Tipping Point* (Gladwell, 2000) proposed what is now a widely accepted phenomenon that "six degrees of separation" allows a connection between any small group of people to the rest of the world. Whilst it may be a powerful concept to know that any one of us is only six contact points away from Barack Obama, Ban Ki-moon, Sting or Madonna, of course this chain is naturally only as strong as its weakest link between the networked groups. The link strength comes from the role that individuals play in their own local networks and not by any group trying to organize itself through links to other networks in support of the six degrees of separation concept – an example of quality rather than quantity perhaps. However, the strength of networking is only fully realized where an individual is known and trusted by the group and, also importantly, where members feel comfortable to make the next connection with another known network with which they have a trusted relationship. Without the attribute of developed trust and acceptance the relationship with another network is likely to fail as the linkage will be immature and possibly regarded as superficial by its network members. On this basis there is a clear message for consultancy marketing: whether from membership of a professional body or in sharing a common leisure interest, **occasional** ad-hoc attendance should **not** be considered as "networking" as it is little more that a preliminary meeting with pleasant, yet reserved, conversation.

Consultants may choose to use their membership of professional bodies and their regular meeting as a good opportunity for networking. These offer two good opportunities: first, before the start of the formal programme and second, immediately after the guest speaker's presentation. In limiting your attendance just to listen to the speaker you will miss out on much of the networking opportunity that the meeting can provide. Skilled networkers arrive in good time and use the expectation of the event as an introduction tool; equally, late departers can make use of the presentation content, speaker's performance, or the announced forthcoming programme as a way to initiate an introduction of themselves to others. The well-known cultural/national distinctions are very obvious in this setting with Kate Fox (2004) observing in her fieldwork research the traditional British reserve which inhibits introductions and a preference for small talk around the weather and local traffic congestion rather than any discussion on business or professional practice topics. This is not to suggest that this is wrong and that networkers should spend the occasion jumping from one conversation to another with a haphazard distribution of their business cards to everyone and asking to let them know of any work offers. For even the most confident of people, this approach is usually inappropriate and should be avoided to save gaining a reputation as being too pushy – or even desperate! Instead, good networkers use the meeting as an opportunity to develop a relationship and then suggest a business meeting for a later date.

For networking to provide a real value it needs to be carefully managed and continually rationalized otherwise individuals run the risk of hoarding a myriad of contacts which are never interactive and can even breed complacency over the need to attend networking events. Furthermore, without such self-imposed management it is possible to develop a false sense of security about personal worth in the marketplace which may also prove to be detrimental to other organizations' and individuals' perceptions of you.

If a networking opportunity either at the earliest stage in the contact cycle or through lack of contact at the latter stages is not adding value then it should be tactfully brought to a close. From a professional work perspective, networking should be considered to be valuable and an essential exercise in both organizational and personal branding; where such brand management and visibility may help to raise your industry profile, credibility and consequently "brand value" – all of which are important characteristics in the management consulting profession.

For some consultants, a professional network is one of their most valuable assets with networking meetings regarded as one of the best ways to continually keep up to date on industrial, commercial and professional developments and to revitalize and grow future business contacts. Whilst many advocate a highly structured approach to networking through contact mapping and customer relationship management frameworks, it is easy to forget to seize those unscripted opportunities which sometimes present themselves as they may prove serendipitous from a future development perspective. Returning to an earlier point, it is the "quality, not quantity" of the networking that in the vast majority of cases produces the best results.

A final word of caution on this topic is that having begun to establish a relationship and perhaps allude to a meeting it is important that this is followed through to show commitment and to begin to engender a degree of trust and reliability. It is also important in a practical way to follow up immediately while the person, the conversation and the issues discussed are fresh in both your minds;

forgetting all about it until the next time the two parties meet is unlikely to progress the relationship or any business opportunity. This leads to the initial exploratory stage and the development of the consultant–client relationship discussed below.

CONSULTANCY SELECTION PROCESS

When a client wishes to engage the services of a consultant there are a number of indicators even at this early stage which may be used in the selection process; based not on price but on the perceived value and relationship with the consultant that the work will involve. The importance of understanding the client's requirements at this early stage is crucial in order to eliminate the risk of failure which may arise from:

- An ill-defined client requirement,
- Poor communication of the problem to be addressed,
- An inappropriate level of expectation, or
- A mismatch between the competencies needed to undertake the work and those of the consultant.

Time spent on this initial understanding will strongly support the successful outcome of the consulting work and assist both parties in developing a fruitful and long-term relationship. A recommended checklist, shown in Figure 2.6, offers benefits to both parties in providing a framework to assist the consultant to understand the

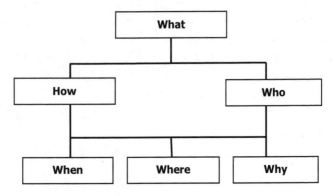

Figure 2.6 Example consultant's checklist format.
From *Managerial Consulting – A Practical Guide*, 2nd edition. C.J. Margerison, 2001. Reproduced with permission of Gower Publishing.

client's business, issues and expectations. This model is taken from Margerson's book on managerial consulting which includes the checklist developed by Sue Morrell of the Queensland State Public Service in Australia. This checklist is not to be used as a step-by-step mechanistic approach to the first meeting but by keeping this approach (What, Who, Why, Where, When and How) in mind it will allow the consultant to explore many of the key issues at the first meeting and gain a full appreciation of the immediate issues and any future working with the client in terms of project delivery. For the consultant the checklist offers a robust approach to understanding the client organization's issues and problems together with constraints, risks and expectations.

What

- What is the background to the request for a project?
- What is the client's system?
- What are the objectives of the project?
- What does the client want from the consultant?
- What information is sought?
- What criteria will be used to measure results?
- What resources (staff, financial, materials) will the client commit to the project?
- What support does the consultant need to carry out the project?
- What checks will be made on progress?

How

- How long will the project take?
- How will the consultant and the project team work?
- How much time will the client commit to the project?
- How will information be communicated?
- How will confidentiality be maintained?

Who

- Who is the client?
- Who will be on the project team?
- Who must agree to the contract?
- Who should be involved in discussions?
- Who should be kept informed of progress?

When

- When will the project start and finish?
- When will the checks on progress occur?

Where

- Where will meetings be held?
- Where will the consultant work?

Why

- Why has the consultant been asked to assist?

Either following the initial meeting, or as part of a formal selection process, the client will have to implement some commercial process leading to an appointment and the award of a contract to undertake the work. For some clients this will follow a typical process as shown in Figure 2.7 which is designed to provide maximum transparency of the appointment process based on a range of selection criteria such as price, methodology, consultancy team, individual skills and competencies, past track record and experience of similar project undertakings and so on. However, this approach is costly and time consuming for both parties and will need to be planned well in advance of the project commencement date which may also be subject to clearance or approval gates during the bidding cycle depending on the sector.

For those consultancy providers with an established working relationship with a client organization, work

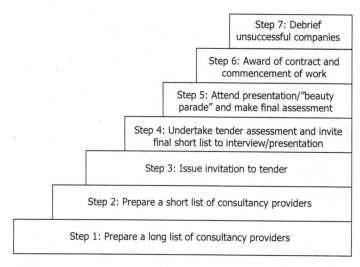

Figure 2.7 Standard appointment process for new consultancy service provider.

may be awarded without the same degree of formal tendering as reflected in the fast-track approach shown in Figure 2.8. Although this offers cost and time benefits for both parties it also demonstrates the importance of maintaining a good relationship between the client and consultant. Indeed, the established level of mutual trust can allow the assignment work to commence in the knowledge that the commercial formal contract will follow later, saving significant service acquisition and delivery.

Figures 2.7 and 2.8 would suggest that consultants should strive to keep close to their clients and reduce the time, cost and effort in gaining new work from competition. Although this clearly provides a financial

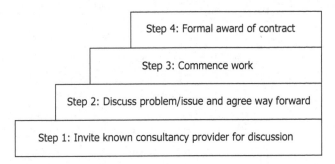

Figure 2.8 Appointment process for consultancy services with established provider.

benefit there are drawbacks for both the client and the consultant in continuing a cosy relationship over a prolonged period of time. Whilst it may be easy for the client to ask the consultant organization to do more work, this may not be in line with the competency (skills, qualifications and experience) of its staff. Not only does this increase the risk of a poor job, it also, over time, dilutes the consultant's independence by being embedded within the client organization and "going native". For the consultant too, repeat work with the same client reduces the future marketability and wider market experience when undertaking new business development especially if the content or scope has not changed.

Having been party to the initial exploratory meeting it is usual for the consulting process to commence formally when the consultant and client are in agreement with the arrangement to work together; this is part of the above appointment processes and is often also Step 1

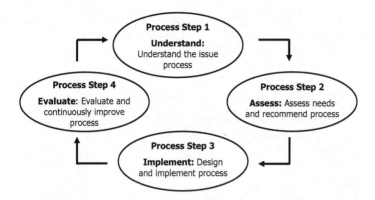

Figure 2.9 The consulting process.
From *High Impact HR: Transforming Human Resources for Competitive Advantage* by Dr David Weiss, 1999. Reproduced with permission of John Wiley and Sons.

of the model shown in Figure 2.9, which illustrates a four stage process of organizational consulting. Although this is presented in a sequential order, the initial consultant and client meeting may have to determine modifications to this in order to suit the business situation and stage of business lifecycle, client requirements, market expectations, stakeholder pressures, resource limitations and time and/or budget constraints, for example.

This model is expanded below to provide more detail for each step.

Process Step 1: Understand the issue process

- Identify the issues through either a proactive approach as a strategic partner to identify opportunities or problems or reactive investigations where a client identifies an opportunity or problem.

- Through conversation about the issue to discover any underlying latent needs.
- Determine consultancy intervention by deciding if you should assess need in depth, implementation and advice and follow-up.

Process Step 2: Assess need and recommend process

- Identify what success would look like for this initiative and the barriers to its success. Identify what is the preferred future for the business, the organization and people processes and the individual and team performance.
- Engage in data collection and analysis through interviews, documentation, surveys, observation and personal experience.
- Identify current reality with individual and team performance, organizational and team processes, and business implications. Determine gaps and recommend direction to address shortfalls. Determine metrics for evaluation of the entire initiative.
- Hold conversation with client on data analysis and recommendation. Propose and agree the next steps.

Process Step 3: Design and implement process

- Prepare design to implement the needs analysis recommendations. Identify metrics for evaluation and secure client approval.

- Communication and formal rollout to the wider business.
- Implement in the simplest way possible, identify "quick hits" and implement recommendations. Consider conducting a pilot project of implementation in more complex situations.
- Implement full project.
- "Roll in" the change to the business so it becomes "business as usual".

Process Step 4: Evaluate and continuously improve process

- Hold conversations with client on desired outcome of evaluation.
- Design overall impact and evaluation analysis.
- Evaluate performance results based on metrics identified and agreed in the proposal.
- Identify the areas of continuous improvement and shared learning and review these with the client.
- Ensure that the project is regarded as part of the normal day-to-day business.
- Prepare close-out report if necessary.

The details of Steps 2 to 4 of David Weiss's Consultancy Process model are also incorporated in the following chapter which covers the management of consultancy projects.

Finally, it has to be remembered that in all of this tendering and development process the consultant should also keep in mind that there may be competition for the work and that this is potentially broader than may be first suggested; the competition may come from:

- Other providers of the same consultancy services.
- Providers of an alternative product or service.
- Other ways of achieving the same required end result.
- Other competitors for the client's budget for the provision of other goods and services.
- The client organization in choosing to adopt your proposal but undertake this from their own resources.
- The client organization using your proposed scope of work, programme and methodology as a basis to engage another service provider to undertake this work.

Such recognition of competition either prompts a reduction or alternatively an increase in the details to the client about methodology, programme, costs, actions and so on in an attempt either to protect the details of their offerings or to promote them more than the competition.

CHAPTER 3

THE MANAGEMENT OF CONSULTANCY PROJECTS

INTRODUCTION

This chapter commences as a continuation of Chapter 2, with an examination of the importance of understanding the client's requirements as the first step in the delivery process from both a consultant's and a client's perspective. It then goes on to consider how treating consultancy assignments as projects can benefit from the traditional project management approach and ends by considering risk management and the role of the consultant.

DEVELOPING THE RELATIONSHIP –
SETTING OFF ON THE RIGHT FOOT

Having developed and implemented a marketing strategy or used networking contacts, an initial exploratory meeting with a potential client may result. As mentioned in Chapter 1, there are many reasons for a client to use a consultant: a search for objectivity or fresh ideas, the requirement for skills and experience not available in the client's organization or simply the need for an extra pair of hands. At the right time and for the right reasons the use of a consulting practice can be invaluable; however, it is suggested that this relationship may be improved in terms of efficiency and effectiveness by investing in preparation from both the consultant and the client for the initial exploratory meeting.

The key to success is for the consultant to fully understand the client's issues, and poor communication of these can result in a dissatisfied client, project failure and even compensation claims. At the start of trying to develop a professional working relationship it has to be said that, as in other areas of life, both parties will need to recognize that a level of reciprocity must exist – in other words, "it takes two to tango". For this suggestion to materialize many clients would benefit by adopting the initial meeting guidelines shown in Figure 3.1.

This is not to suggest here that all the fault of a failed project arises from the client's ill-defined brief. Having looked at the initial meeting from a client's perspective, Figure 3.2 then offers some prompts for the consultant

	Main advice to a client	Details of advice
1	Be clear on the purpose, scope and objectives of the task.	Clients should be clear on the scope, purpose and objectives of the task being asked of the consultant and what they want the consultancy to deliver. This is not to suggest that it's all down to the client as the sign of a good consultant is one who has the enthusiasm to help the client clearly define the scope of the task, while placing the client's interests ahead of their own. Without this initial understanding of the objectives of the consultancy assignment it will be difficult to envision what a successful outcome will be for the client organization.
2	Choose a style of working which best suits your organization/project.	There are a number of ways consultants can be used depending on your circumstances, ranging from reimbursable secondments into your office, lump sum work packages, agreed limit of liability draw-down arrangements to full risk–reward outsourced service level arrangements. The approach should be structured to achieve the level of control and accountability that both the client and consultant are comfortable with and include a suitable exit strategy and closure if the consultant relationship does not deliver the expected results and also as a handover on completion of the consultant's work.
3	Know what you are looking for.	Clients should be clear how they will judge the success of the consultant's work against specific and transparent criteria. This will also help to establish what results they are looking for and provides a platform for sharing a common understanding with the consultant. As a result, the consultant is much more likely to deliver what the client wants and equally importantly **when** it is wanted.
4	Utilize the consultant's process.	Through the consultant's experience of having delivered many different assignments for clients across a range of disciplines and industries, they should have evolved a series of tried and tested approaches which will allow them to reach a satisfactory conclusion. (This experience is often the basis for their appointment – so use it). It should be noted by both parties that past experience should not just be repeated again and again as circumstances, cultures, and business requirements change and what worked well in one sector may not be fully transferable into another. If the client thinks it's as easy as this, then perhaps buying the book instead of hiring an expensive resource may be a better solution. Clients should also have some confidence that the consultant is appropriately tailoring its services to meet their specific requirements.
5	Provide lots of feedback.	Good consultants should be very focused on customer satisfaction. However, communication is a two-way process and clients should let them know what they are doing well and what they can improve on. This feedback will help ensure the consultant delivers what the client wants and, in the longer term, will help them adapt to serve the client better in the future. It is also recommended that the client should have contact with a senior person in the consulting company to help handle any sensitive issues which may arise.
6	Develop a long-term relationship with your consultant.	The more a client works with the same consulting company, the more the experience allows the consultant to understand the client organization and culture (and vice versa). This longer-term relationship can benefit both parties in many ways. Even when a consultant is serving others, he/she is gathering new skills and experiences which may be of benefit to you on future tasks. The optimum client/consultancy working arrangements for a particular activity must be determined on a case-by-case basis. It is in the interests of both parties to get these arrangements right. Often the consultant will have more experience of what works well and what doesn't and on this basis the client should seek their advice at an early stage and develop these arrangements together.
7	Expect the consultant to have a methodology for the consultancy process – not just the task	Naturally, clients select and appoint consultants based on their track record, experience, etc. which they can draw upon for the benefit of the client organization. However, clients should also expect a structured approach to the initial meeting with the consultant using a systematic process to fully understand the assignment brief – rather than just asking random questions on the spur of the moment.

Figure 3.1 Advice to clients at project commencement.

	Main advice to consultant	Details of advice
1	Relevant communications.	Listen to what is being told and for what is not mentioned. Base questions and initiate a discussion around the topics that concern the client – not your track record – and be aware of latent needs and risks.
2	Understanding of problem.	Demonstrate that you understand the key issues involved and how they may be managed. Provide examples and suggestions for the client to consider. Show empathy in the situation which the client is describing, particularly with respect to managing some of the issues and concerns around the introduction of new processes, organization structures and performance requirements from a change programme.
3	Understanding of industry sector.	Show an understanding for the client's industry, market sector, and competitive position, a simple SWOT analysis can be a good starting point on which to demonstrate some knowledge and engage with the client.
4	Questioning for clarity.	Focus your questions to understand the client's problem and requirements and offer a relevant approach based on understanding and previous experience or track record. However, be aware that many clients consider themselves to be "unique" and simply do not want a standard approach to their issues or a direct copy of what you have done elsewhere.
5	Offer initial approaches not a final solution.	Do not be afraid to challenge assumptions and offer alternatives for the client's consideration. Here a range of approaches that may be discussed with the client demonstrates not only a depth of your knowledge and credibility but also this may present the opportunity through discussion to start to develop a good working relationship. (Note that the book *The Essential Management Toolbox* was written specifically for this purpose.)
6	Development of relationship.	Seek to develop a trusting relationship, whilst this will usually take time it can also be demonstrated by actions such as provision of additional information, past examples of work (case studies), loan of publications on specific issues relative to the work. Note that this point also relates to ethical behaviour covered in Chapter 1 as this needs to be carefully managed. Do not ever share confidential information or indeed criticize other clients in their approach or business operations. The client should be very cautious about trusting you with knowledge of their operations if you share this openly with others without their agreement. Often it is usual for both parties to have a confidentiality or non-disclosure agreement as part of the formal engagement process.
7	Culture.	Show respect for the client's culture, this may be both organizational culture and indeed national, ethnic and religious persuasion especially in international locations. This is not to suggest that consultants need to be experts on the fine details of every country's culture but an overall appreciation of the political, economic, social, legal and religious pressures will be very valuable to show the necessary level of respect. (Note that the UK Foreign and Commonwealth website is a good source of useful information.)
8	Enthusiasm.	If you are not enthusiastic about assisting the client with its requirements then do not be disappointed if you are not selected or are regarded as only working on the task just for the income or until another more interesting job opportunity emerges.
9	Next steps.	Explain that the success of the consultancy assignment is not in the initial research, reporting, or in making recommendations but in its implementation. Whilst this may be beyond the scope of the consultancy assignment currently being described, it may be an important point that, having made the recommendations, the consultants are also available to assist with the implementation of the findings. Consultants who produce glossy reports, take their fees and walk away from standing by their recommendations may find that they have limited repeat business.
10	Project issues of time, cost and quality.	Whilst for many individuals the issue of payment is often left undefined, consultants do need the commercial terms agreed in advance of engagement in most cases. Establishing an agreed fee rate, a method for progress reporting, a method for satisfying any client audit requirements such as timesheets, etc., report quality control and expected timescales will all benefit the relationship from the outset and allow it to progress on the right professional terms.

Figure 3.2 Advice to consultants at project commencement.

to consider in order to extract the required information and facilitate an early contribution to a fledgling project.

CONSULTANCY AS A PROJECT

It is proposed that consultancy assignments should be considered to be "projects" in that they usually have a defined start, middle and end; if they do not, then the consultant is more likely to be used as an additional resource for the business rather than as a specialist to improve the client organization's overall business performance through a set of advisory activities and implementation actions. This is not to say that there is no role for such top-up resources when business demand dictates but this ideally should be part of a client's deliberate resourcing policy rather than as expensive and often reactive "body-shop" arrangements from a consultancy service provider.

On the basis that consultancy assignments may be regarded as "projects", the techniques employed in project management, although normally used in large-scale and often complex undertakings, are well suited to guide the consultant to the successful completion of their assignment with a client. The widely accepted understanding that the main variables in any project are time, cost and quality shown in Figure 3.3 are discussed below together with the project management skill of being able to balance these variables to the satisfaction of their clients.

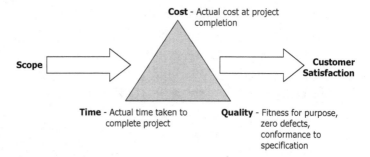

Figure 3.3 Project management variables.
From *The Essential Management Toolbox: Tools, Models and Notes for Managers and Consultants*. S.A. Burtonshaw-Gunn, 2008.

Time: Before appointment – and in fact generally as part of the selection criteria – the consultant will have gained some understanding of the requirements and constraints of undertaking the work for this specific client in terms of the time and effort required and often from an outline programme of the key actions. Typically at the outset of the assignment, the completion date for the work will usually need to be agreed with the client and whilst for some interventions this will be of a short duration, for others of a more substantial nature this will be longer to reflect the level of work to be undertaken. Naturally, for both parties the goal will be to complete the work in line with the agreed programme timescales, although due to appropriate circumstances which may prevent completion to programme, time extensions will need to be agreed in advance. It is suggested, however, that by utilizing a project management approach to gain a detailed understanding of the tasks to be addressed the need for an extension can often be eliminated. For example, even the production of a simple programme will prompt the consultant to list the key tasks and milestone deliverables such as research, analysis, report writing, implementation planning, etc. On this basis a timeframe for each of the activities can be allocated and hence considerations of the respective amount of work content for each to ensure that this is a feasible undertaking. In addition, through this planning exercise it will be possible to target a completion date ahead of that "officially" required to permit a small contingency allowance to be built in for any unplanned events which may not necessarily be directly related to the consultancy process. Such a programme should also provide the client with a degree of confidence that the consultant is addressing the task in a professional manner by demonstrating how the project will be undertaken. Having developed a realistic programme the consultant can use it throughout the assignment period to monitor and report progress at each stage of the data gathering and report production activities.

Cost: From a project management point of view, historically many large-scale projects have suffered from cost over-runs mostly because of technical interface difficulties that could not have been foreseen at the outset of the project. For the management consultant the number of interfaces is often relatively few and mostly these are confined to the client's organization respondents for questionnaires and/or interviews involved in the collection of field data. To a large extent these can therefore be assumed to be within the consultant's direct control. Any research costs such as benchmarking, travel, access to data, etc. are likely to be at a very low cost relative to the overall fees.

Quality: In the case of the quality of the work, this will need to meet the requirements of the client and this adherence largely determines the success of the investment in the work undertaken. Again, the lesson drawn from conventional project management experience is that there is no point in completing a major undertaking whether on time and/or within budget if it does not do what it is supposed to. Similarly, the consultant's work must meet the requirements laid down in any QA process that the consultant is working to. From the consulting perspective the consultant should view the term "quality" to be the production of a piece of work to a high standard through the use of appropriate language, structure, format, presentation and articulation of the findings of the assignment undertaken. A subjective quality assessment will often focus on the consultant's ability to link sections of the assignment report to develop a comprehensive and supportable set of conclusions and recommendations from the work conducted.

Quality should be part of the working arrangement not just in the acceptance and implementation of the final report but from the outset in finding out exactly what the client's expectations are and developing a trusting working relationship throughout the assignment process. This is also seen in the client having confidence in the individual and his/her team, and importantly feeling that they are credible and able to make a valued contribution.

Having examined the three project management components of time, cost and quality, the consultant cannot rely on just balancing these three variables – difficult as this task is – to please the client without regular contact and progress reporting. This communication is important to show that the work is progressing towards meeting the required quality and business expectations. Indeed, the benefits of such two-way communications are twofold:

- First, to allow the client to gain a level of confidence that the work being undertaken remains achievable in both technical and practicable terms.
- Second, to provide to the consultant access to the client as an informed sounding board for discussing uncertainties and seeking operational business clarification.

From the consultant's perspective, maintaining close contact with their client through the assignment period should minimize the possibility of failure on grounds of quality especially as the required standard will have been discussed, better understood and client expectations managed. In the event of poor performance on grounds of quality an amount of rework will be necessary and this will inevitably erode any contingency and may even require extra time by the consultant resulting in a delay in the client's implementation phase of the project.

In looking at the construction industry where project management is extensively used, failure – even at the final stage of a project – on grounds of quality may be recoverable with additional work, although this will often necessitate an extension to the programme with a corresponding increase in the overall costs. Often this situation would not have arisen with a thorough understanding of the client's requirements and with more regular communication on progress. It is therefore stressed that regular and planned consultant and client communications on the project scope, progress and findings will reduce the risk of project failure. Furthermore it should be noted that the other element of the model (Figure 3.3) is that of "Scope" which is required to be fully understood at the earliest opportunity – ideally before the actual start of the consultancy work – as this is paramount to the success of a consultancy intervention being focused on delivering the required business outcomes. Whilst the accepted three project management variables described above can be seen to be applicable to many consultancy assignments, specifically those involved in the production of feasibility and options studies, the importance of fully understanding the scope of work needs to be explored and agreed with the client as soon as practicable.

RISK MANAGEMENT AND THE ROLE OF THE CONSULTANT

This section looks at the subject of risk management from a project, business or operational viewpoint where such risks can be internally or externally driven and may impact on a consultancy project's stated scope, schedule and cost objectives. Risk management can be used in helping to test the validity of client requirements and should be integral in developing the consultancy scope of work. Figure 3.4 shows a range of benefits that risk management may offer and although all will not be applicable to every consultancy project, a number of these will be.

Risk management has evolved into a formal systematic process to become a subset of project management and should be regarded as a means of dealing with uncertainty, identifying sources of uncertainty and the risks associated with them, and then managing those risks so that any identified negative outcomes are minimized (or avoided altogether), and any positive outcomes are capitalized upon.

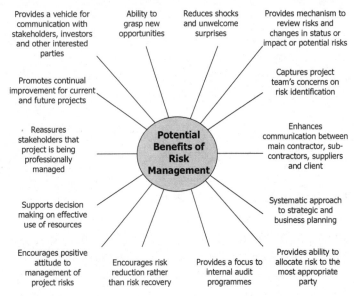

Figure 3.4 Benefits of risk management.
From *Risk and Financial Management in Construction*, S.A. Burtonshaw-Gunn, 2009. Reproduced with kind permission from Gower Publications.

The need to manage uncertainty is inherent in most projects of any size and significance which require a formal project management approach. In considering risk management and the role of the consultant, it should be noted that risk management cannot be owned by one individual on the project as all team members must be both "risk aware" and participate in activities to improve a project's stability and predictability of performance outcome. The two objectives for the deployment of the discipline of risk management are:

- To plan and take management action to achieve the aims of removing or reducing the likelihood and effects of risks before they occur and dealing with actual problems when they do; and
- To continuously monitor potential impacts of risks, review the associated actions, and to provide managed adequate financial and schedule contingencies for risks should they occur.

To be fully effective, management consultants will need to recognize that risks exist and actively manage them. This should be viewed as an indication of good project management and not an admission of failure. By looking ahead at the potential events that may impact the project and putting actions in place to address them (where appropriate), project teams can proactively manage risks and increase the chances of successfully delivering the project within the planned time, cost and quality project requirements. Whilst risk management may be a proactive approach it cannot control future events but will allow decisions to be made and actions taken if such identified risks become reality. On the basis of such an understanding of what can go wrong a number of actions are open to both the consultant and the client to manage the risk where, to a large extent, the response will be a function of the probability and quantified impact of the risk occurring.

Although the way risk management is operationalized varies from one company to another, one common

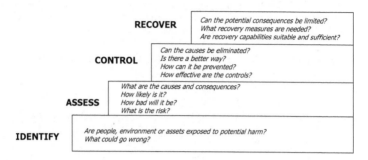

Figure 3.5   Common steps in a risk management process.
From *Risk and Financial Management in Construction*, S.A. Burtonshaw-Gunn, 2009. Reproduced with kind permission from Gower Publications.

approach is a staged process of risk identification followed by deployment of a number of strategies for its management. To support this process there are a number of common risk management steps; however, in general, many follow a similar basic approach of risk identification, assessment, controlled response and finally risk recovery as shown in Figure 3.5.

Clearly, it is not possible to control all risks but to ignore them and any mitigation actions will undoubtedly lead to adverse consequences for the project should these materialize. The consequences of failing to deal effectively with risk will not only jeopardize the client's work but for the consultant will also include a loss of credibility and possibly personal or organizational liability and fines. Other important consequences of failing to manage risk are the potential for significant cost over-runs, an inability to achieve desired project technical objective(s), schedule delays, project de-scoping and ultimately in extreme circumstances project cancellation. All of which are likely to lead to unhappy clients and a significant reduction for the consultancy provider in future project opportunities with the same client.

In addressing risk management within the lifecycle of a consultancy project, this should use a risk planning process to cover both known and unknown risks with respect to the project undertaking. Whilst the response to known risks is typically proactive, managed, planned and budgeted for, the response to unknown risks, on the other hand, is often reactive, unmanaged, not budgeted or resourced, and often encourages further unplanned reactions. Many organizations in commerce, industry and the public sector are well suited to the use of risk-based decision making, which provides a framework for the typical risk management process as shown in Figure 3.6. Successfully applied risk-based decision making can be both powerful and cost effective.

The steps in the risk management process begin by identifying the potential risk and recording this in a formal way; this is followed by an assessment of the risks looking to qualify and quantify the risk against a set of consistent criteria to determine the risk significance and the means for managing its consequences. The extent of assessment and documentation will be dependent on the significance of the proposed change and is likely to range from assessment based on:

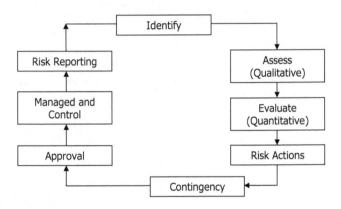

Figure 3.6 Risk management process.
From *Risk and Financial Management in Construction*, S.A. Burtonshaw-Gunn 2009. Reproduced with kind permission from Gower Publications.

- past experience;
- parametric comparison;
- knowledge of the client's requirements and its culture;
- comprehensive numerical assessment depending on the complexity of the project; and
- the cost, time and quality impact of the risk occurring.

Following the identification and analysis of the risks, the options available to address these will be based on one or more of the "4Ts" risk response actions: Terminate, Treat, Tolerate, Transfer as shown in the model of Figure 3.7.

In addition to the above 4Ts risk response actions is the additional option of rejecting the risk if it is considered that the occurrence of the risk is so improbable that it will not be a threat to the client's project.

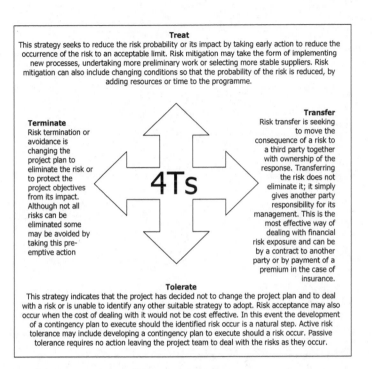

Treat
This strategy seeks to reduce the risk probability or its impact by taking early action to reduce the occurrence of the risk to an acceptable limit. Risk mitigation may take the form of implementing new processes, undertaking more preliminary work or selecting more stable suppliers. Risk mitigation can also include changing conditions so that the probability of the risk is reduced, by adding resources or time to the programme.

Terminate
Risk termination or avoidance is changing the project plan to eliminate the risk or to protect the project objectives from its impact. Although not all risks can be eliminated some may be avoided by taking this pre-emptive action

4Ts

Transfer
Risk transfer is seeking to move the consequence of a risk to a third party together with ownership of the response. Transferring the risk does not eliminate it; it simply gives another party responsibility for its management. This is the most effective way of dealing with financial risk exposure and can be by a contract to another party or by payment of a premium in the case of insurance.

Tolerate
This strategy indicates that the project has decided not to change the project plan and to deal with a risk or is unable to identify any other suitable strategy to adopt. Risk acceptance may also occur when the cost of dealing with it would not be cost effective. In this event the development of a contingency plan to execute should the identified risk occur is a natural step. Active risk tolerance may include developing a contingency plan to execute should a risk occur. Passive tolerance requires no action leaving the project team to deal with the risks as they occur.

Figure 3.7 Strategies for risk response.
From *Risk and Financial Management in Construction*, S.A. Burtonshaw-Gunn, 2009. Reproduced with kind permission from Gower Publications.

Following these risk strategies an evaluation of the risk response options can be undertaken taking into account their cost, benefits and the views of the client and other relevant stakeholders. Whilst this process is reasonably straightforward in principle, in practice there can be demanding issues to overcome, for example:

- Ensuring the options have been properly selected and defined.
- Setting assessment criteria, and objectives and their relative importance.
- Identifying risk issues and perceptions.
- Assessing the performance of options against aspects that may not be quantifiable, or which may involve judgements and perceptions that vary or are open to interpretation.
- Dealing with differences in the uncertainties of estimates, data and analyses.
- Managing or avoiding hidden assumptions or biases.

In considering risk management in consultancy projects, knowledge of the client's culture will assist in providing synergy between the individual capability and the organization's set performance targets. This knowledge should be used to drive, inform and support planning and from this overview of risk management it should be seen that effective risk management can:

- Anticipate and influence events before they happen by taking a proactive approach.
- Provide knowledge and information about predicted events.
- Inform and, where possible, improve the quality of decision making, recognizing the preferred hierarchy of risk avoidance, risk reduction, risk control and risk acceptance.

- Avoid assumptions and false definition of risks.
- Make the project management process open and transparent.
- Assist in the delivery of project objectives in terms of quality, time and cost targets.
- Prompt consideration of making contingency plans.
- Provide auditable records of risk planning and risk control.
- Demonstrate to the client that the work is being professionally managed.

To achieve effective and efficient risk management the commonest approach is for consultants to make this an integral part of their consultancy project plan.

CHAPTER 4

MANAGEMENT CONSULTANCY DELIVERY

INTRODUCTION

Whilst it is impossible to describe the delivery details applicable to every consultancy assignment, this chapter concentrates on the essential delivery activities undertaken by consultants across a wide number of consultancy projects. Key to the success of these activities is knowing what is required to deliver the desired outcomes for the client and selecting a methodology best aligned with

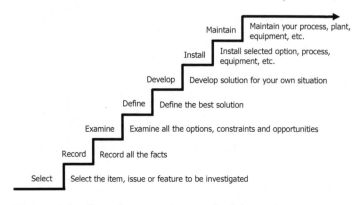

Figure 4.1 Consultancy project methodology.
From *The Essential Management Toolbox: Tools, Models and Notes for Managers and Consultants*, S.A. Burtonshaw-Gunn, 2008.

these criteria. One model which is useful to set the scene of what the consultant undertaking and role will be – and sometimes that of the client too – is shown in Figure 4.1 which follows a conventional structured approach to the work.

As seen in the above model this is broad enough to be used in a large range of consulting opportunities commencing with understanding the issues and problems to reporting, recommending and implementing changes to suit the client's requirements. A feature of this model is its extension beyond the undertaking to the longer-term maintenance of the proposed systems and hence a link to continuous improvement. The consultancy project methodology also provides a natural link to the topics within this chapter commencing with research, problem solving, workshop facilitation to either examine problems or test proposed solutions, and finally a look at how the work undertaken may be reported.

UNDERTAKING RESEARCH

Many management consultancy assignments involve an element of collecting information and research within the business environment and as such it would be odd to find a company that did not undertake research or require some kind of data collection whether in gaining customer satisfaction results or by taking proactive steps to understand market performance and product development. Without doubt there can be no set method or approach to undertaking research as it is often unique to the company's objectives and consequently needs tailoring to the industry under review, the amount of time available and budget limitations. However, there are a number of options open for data collection such as the collection of primary data from interviews, questionnaires, focus groups, surveys and so on to secondary data collection from desktop studies, benchmarking visits to other organizations and literature reviews. There is a range of deployable research strategies which are available but these need to be aligned to the research objectives to achieve optimum value. These are shown in Figure 4.2. The feature of this model is the relationship between the size

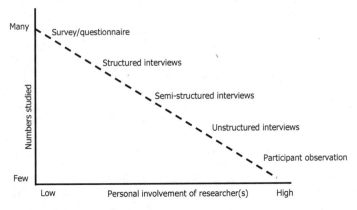

Figure 4.2   Research strategies.
Graph of "Researcher involvement" (page 89) from *The New Introducing Sociology*, edited by Peter Worsley. First published as *Introducing Sociology*, Penguin Books 1970. Third edition published as *The New Introducing Sociology*, 1987, 1992. Copyright © Peter Worsley and contributors 1970, 1977, 1987, 1992.

of the research scope and the individuals involved compared to the amount of consultant time available.

The choice of strategy may be a combination of what is appropriate for the client and the data to be collected, or as a compromise between the ideal research strategy and the project management variables of time, cost and quality as discussed in Chapter 3.

Undertaking research can be used to make process improvements, obtain customer feedback and finally provide clear linkage to problem identification and resolution, or declared business objectives. The involvement of the consultant is also of key importance as this provides guidance on their research involvement ranging from interviews, questionnaires, surveys to observation and more direct involvement. In addition to the ways that data may be collected is the consideration of a wider framework approach open to researchers such as experiential case studies, action research, historical documentation and experimentation. Of course, collecting the raw data is often regarded as the most interesting part of any research but careful consideration also needs to be undertaken before this stage so that the "right" data is collected and a plan of how this data will be analysed is in place, recognizing the scale of the task and volume of data. This analysis can cover either a qualitative or quantitative approach or both of these as they should not be regarded as being mutually exclusive – good research rarely relies on just one approach to the exclusion of the other. The attributes of each of the qualitative and quantitative approaches are provided below. Quantitative data in business research settings has attractions because it uses numbers and can present findings in the form of graphs and tables; it conveys a sense of solid, objective research and can be easier to demonstrate "bottom line" impacts. Colin Robson in his book *Real World Research* (2002) suggests that quantitative research can be used if:

- You believe that there is an objective reality that can be measured.
- Your audience is familiar with or supportive of quantitative studies.

- The research question is confirmatory or predictive.
- The available literature is relatively large.
- The research focus covers a lot of breadth.
- The time available is relatively short.
- Your ability/desire to work with people is medium to low.
- Your desire to structure is high.
- You have skills in the area(s) of statistics and deductive reasoning.
- Your writing skills are strong in the area of technical, scientific writing.

On the other hand, qualitative data, whether words or images, may be more applicable and is often the product of a process of interpretation. The consultant may undertake qualitative research as a means to increase understanding by careful analysis and interpretation. Again Robson suggests that qualitative research may be undertaken if:

- You believe that there are multiple constructed realities.
- The audience is familiar with/supportive of qualitative studies.
- The research question is exploratory, interpretative.
- The available literature is limited or missing.
- The research focus involves in-depth study.
- The time available is relatively long.
- Your ability/desire to work with people is high.
- Your desire to structure is low.

- You have skills in attention to detail and inductive reasoning.
- Your writing skills are strong in the area of literary or narrative writing.

In the business environment the focus of the research, for example, may be on customer views, perceptions and needs and is less likely to require a review of any secondary data from the published literature to support the findings. Undertaking research will mostly require this to be documented for the client and is likely to feature as part of the consultant's report. Whilst report writing is covered as a topic in this chapter it should be noted that research work is typically documented as an appendix or separate annex to the main consultant's report although the main document of the report will make clear reference to key research findings.

PROBLEM SOLVING AND DECISION MAKING

Management consultants often have to assist managers and indeed organizations in decision making which is usually linked to problem resolution to aid performance enhancement. There are a number of different styles of decision making from which to choose centred around the involvement of other people in the decision-making process. The topic of decision making and problem resolution may be initiated as a reaction to internal and external influences or, on the other hand, as a proactive approach to continuous improvement and lean thinking such as the adoption of Rudyard Kipling's "six honest serving men" as an aid to systematically questioning operations with a view to making business improvement actions (see also Chapter 5). Apart from using a problem resolution process to address issues it can also give rise to innovative solutions and encourage creativity. One of the most useful management consultancy tools in support of problem resolution is the Ishakawa or "fishbone" diagram (Figure 4.3) which can be very powerful when used in engaging groups to identify and link common business problem issues, operational drivers and then seek solutions

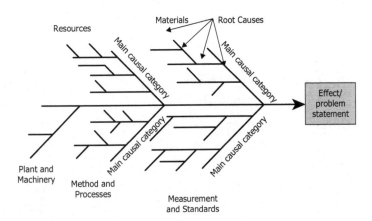

Figure 4.3 Fishbone diagram.
From *The Essential Management Toolbox: Tools, Models and Notes for Managers and Consultants*, S.A. Burtonshaw-Gunn, 2008.

to each significant problem area. The strength of this cause and effect fishbone model comes from the use of visualization which promotes a shared understanding of the issues and leads ultimately to diagnosis and group ownership of the proposed solutions to the problem. Whilst the fishbone approach is generally centred around set areas (typically materials, resources, machinery and so on), another free-form method applicable at group or individual level to creative thinking is the use of mind mapping. This is a highly visual graphical technique deployed through colours, pictures, numbers and net-worked linkages to stimulate arranging ideas and their interconnections which develops related thoughts that may lead to creative ideas.

It should be noted that for over the last decade or so, with a move towards a closer supplier–buyer collabo-rative working arrangement, many businesses have estab-lished a problem resolution process prior to any problems being identified so that when a problem does emerge both parties know what processes they should use to address it. Decision making and problem resolution should not just be considered to be a process to be deployed when issues need to be addressed but also as a proactive way to promote innovation and stimulate creativity within the learning organization. The tools of decision making such as the fishbone diagram and the Force Field Analysis developed by the German born social scientist Kurt Lewin work well in facilitated work-shops as they offer clear understanding of the driving and

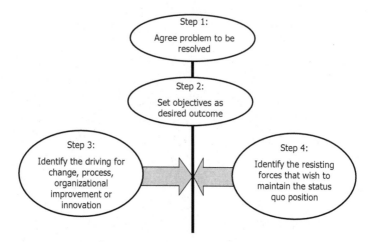

Figure 4.4 Development of a Force Field Analysis.
From *The Essential Management Toolbox: Tools, Models and Notes for Managers and Consultants*, S.A. Burtonshaw-Gunn, 2008.

resisting forces and can prompt challenges, discussion and rational solutions. Figure 4.4 shows the development of a Force Field Model which can be used to encourage groups to visualize the problem in terms of a balance between those forces which drive a change and those of resistance. The steps involved in its construction lend themselves to group work with opportunities for discussion of each issue and how the removal of barriers identified can best be managed.

The forces for and against a change can be a catalyst for a new process to be introduced, new ways of working, new production development, new target market or a new business strategy. These forces can appear on both sides of the force field which typically can include forces such as:

- People, team or individuals.
- Organizational structure.
- Product or services delivery.
- Technological changes.
- Financial targets or constraints.
- The power of suppliers, customers or competitors (see also Figure 5.2).
- The PESTLE elements (see also Figure 5.4).

These can be used to identify the forces (also shown in Figure 4.5); some of these will prevent the change and some will assist it. The model is good for identifying these forces and allowing an assessment to be made on addressing them.

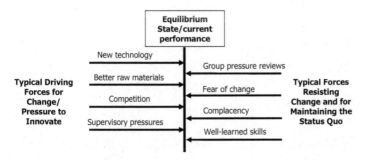

Figure 4.5 Example of populated Force Field Analysis.
From *The Essential Management Toolbox: Tools, Models and Notes for Managers and Consultants*, S.A. Burtonshaw-Gunn, 2008.

WORKSHOP FACILITATION

Within the larger organizations there is a growing acceptance of shared development through the use of group
facilitation which can often be linked to business continuous improvement or as part of a change management
process. The facilitation role may be delivered as part of
an internal corporate communication style or increasingly
as part of a consultant/client relationship. The term
"workshop" has itself emerged over the last decade or so
to describe such a working group event although this
term is not universally recognizable and some local
knowledge is needed as to its applicability in some countries as the term when translated may portray the wrong
meaning.

While there is a choice of using internal or external
facilitators the aim will be to bring key decision makers
together in order to gain "buy-in" by a group to a new
process, organizational change or product development.
The key to the success of a workshop is predominantly
a product of the preparation in knowing who is attend-
ing, who is able to make decisions or hinder the group's
progress, what the workshop objectives are and finally
what a successful outcome will consist of. The roles that
need to be undertaken by the consultant as a workshop
facilitator are outlined below as it is not just the matter
of running a group meeting as this task demands specific
facilitation skills and techniques such as:

- **Leadership:** Having the ability to move from a directive, hierarchical mode of operating through cooperation to an autonomous, standing back mode, depending upon the maturity level of the team and the demands of the specific situation at the time.
- **Discussion management:** Able to manage a discussion and all forms of communication through the use of appropriate interpersonal skills. This includes creating a safe environment for people to fully participate, both when agreeing and disagreeing. Skills needed include active listening, questioning, summarizing, linking and reflecting, along with self-disclosure when appropriate.
- **Structures (including tools and techniques):** Having a range of structures available and with an understanding of their suitability, effect and operation. This also covers tools for decision making and action planning. (The book *The Essential Management Toolbox* presents many tools and models for managers and consultants, which may be useful for wider workshop involvement.)

Workshop attendees according to Nick Eve's facilitation course can be categorized into the following four groups:

Passenger: This attendee is like being on a train travelling through interesting places with their feet up, enjoying the ride. They are protected from weather and local conditions, and as such like the journey but are not actively engaged. They like looking out of the window and taking a back seat.

Protester: As this suggests the person is unhappy about being present and is voicing this dissatisfaction volubly. Often this is to do with outside pressures either at work or at home. There is the feeling that they should not be there as it's the wrong time, wrong place, the wrong content, etc.

Prisoner: This person is like a "protestor" only the dissent is less voluble. There is a sense of resignation, an acceptance that they are present but they only intend to give their "name, rank and number". This may be due to time of day, hunger, a need for a break or the feeling that a particular exercise or item has gone on for too long.

Participant: This person is actively engaged in the event with their head, heart and body; they are interested and stimulated by what is coming. They want to be at the event and are keen to take part fully in whatever occurs to get as much as possible from the experience.

Against this background a programme for the workshop can be developed and whilst the nature of workshops is typically semi-structured to accommodate discussion, problem resolution, idea generation and to some degree an amount of deviation, the importance of a workshop plan is to guide the facilitator in meeting the workshop objectives.

Workshops are like projects in that they too have a start, middle and end and can often have a high opportunity cost attached to attendance. The start may be at the time of the workshop, or before in the case of some pre-workshop preparation, reading, questionnaire completion, etc. Starting the workshop correctly is important as this sets the scene of what is expected in the form of output, participation and group "rules" of operating. Again the level of individual participation and involvement will vary in different cultures and this will need to be reflected in the workshop design. Attendance at workshops is governed largely by the topic and the required level of involvement of the participants: some workshop topics are only effective in small groups where more time is available to get to know each other and where a large degree of flexibility is needed. On the other hand, large group facilitation offers other advantages in bringing ideas forward, promoting wide involvement and in seeking to identify overlaps or shortfalls. Some practical guidance for facilitating both small and large groups is provided in Figure 4.6.

Many of the tools and models are used at workshops to stimulate discussion, explore new ideas, prompt the sharing of experience or utilize ready-proven techniques for adoption, such as in decision making and problem resolution. Facilitated workshops can be used to support a number of areas of management such as change management initiatives; process improvement; business planning at corporate and/or functional levels; and organizational development.

Guidelines	Advice
For facilitating small groups of 4 to 12 attendees.	Always have in mind the task of the group and if necessary periodically remind the group of it.
	The leader is there to promote communication, not as the fount of all knowledge.
	Avoid introducing too much material; encourage personal contributions above mere intellectual knowledge.
	Encourage personal contributions by sharing views and feelings, especially group feelings.
	Try to use silences creatively.
	Be wary of the cosy "united" group and encourage creative dissent.
	Watch for openings for the silent members.
	Be firm, but caring, with the dominant member(s).
	Encourage group members generally to own feelings and opinions, rather than make one person appear unusual.
	Try to balance the needs of the individuals and the needs of the group.
	Make clear and definite arrangements about time, frequency and place.
	Consider the right size of a group, and the balance of its membership.
	Always consider the feelings engendered by changes of membership.
	Bosses (and other authority figures): beware of your presence in the group.
For facilitating large groups of more than 12 attendees.	Balance the limitations on communication with the advantage of spread of opinion.
	Try to arrange seating so that people can see and hear each other.
	Do not be taken in by the passivity of many or the accomplished words of the few.
	Encourage the expression of clear, simple views.
	Do not become trapped in legislative procedures.
	Discourage "them" and "us" slogans.
	Be wary as a facilitator of accepting the "messianic" role.
	Reflect back accurately from one part of the group to another.
	Demonstrate in your own contributions how you wish others to communicate to the large group.
	Respond to individual contributions.
	Clarify points of difference, summing up different aspects of discussion as the meeting proceeds.
	Clarify the agenda under discussion and rules for voting or decision making.
	Provide clear leadership without dictating the outcome of discussion.
	Clarify what is reasonable for a large group to discuss and decide. Use small groups in conjunction with the large group.
	Facilitate large groups with least one other leader.

Figure 4.6 Guidelines for facilitating groups.
From Michael Jacobs, *Swift to Hear – Facilitating Skills in Listening and Responding*, 2000. Reproduced by permission of SPCK Publishing.

DELIVERABLES

On completion of the consultancy assignment, or even part-way through, it is usual to produce a report to the client; this may be a written document or a presentation. Both of these are a feature of stand-alone one-day training programmes or as part of many larger consultancy development programmes. This is a pivotal element of management consulting and the key points of both report writing and presentations are discussed below.

Report Writing

It would be unusual to find consultancy assignments which do not result in a written report of some form on how the consultancy project has been undertaken, its objectives and how these have been satisfied. For the consultant, as the report author, this would usually follow their preferred consultancy organization style or adhere to a preference from the client particularly if the report is be to transmitted to another party, agency or government body. Depending on the nature of the project the content will differ; in general terms, however, consultancy reports follow a similar format, namely:

- **Executive summary:** This is usually limited to one or two pages which are often presented in bullet point format.

- **Introduction:** This sets the scene regarding what has prompted the work and hence this report and its recommendations.
- **Scope of work and any limitations:** This will clarify the extent of the work undertaken, whether it is to address a local, regional, national or international problem for the client organization.
- **Methodology or approach:** This section will provide some confidence that the data has been collected in an appropriate way, who was involved, the basis for their involvement, how the data was collected and the sample size selected. Without this description the basis of the findings and the subsequent recommendations are more likely to be open to question.
- **Findings:** This is a presentation of the facts from the study made in a logical sequence and in an unbiased manner.
- **Conclusions:** These are made after the analysis of the facts and should be presented in the report with a supporting explanation. Logical conclusions based upon a number of facts are generally straightforward and immediately acceptable, but if experience and judgement are included, this should be stated.
- **Recommendations:** These must be based on the findings and conclusions and prescribed in a cogent manner. It is often helpful to present these as short-, medium- and long-term actions.
- **References:** Where reference material has been used this should be noted as this provides the client with

some surety that the consultant has sought to examine other industry, section or relation examples from published works rather than basing the entire report solely on more limited knowledge and experience.

- **Supporting information:** Where information is used in the main body of the text it may be useful to provide the raw data as an appendix. Where key information also exists but is more of a supplementary nature this may be included as a separate annex.

In order to keep control of the report from a quality assurance and indeed from a professional standards point of view, the report is usually given a unique number and is signed by the author and/or lead consultant as representing accurately the work undertaken. This also provides some confidence to the client that the recommendations are professionally endorsed. In order for the consultancy assignment to be regarded as successful the report must be considered to be a project deliverable and comply with the project management variables previously discussed; specifically, it should reflect the three project characteristics in the following way:

Time: The report must be planned for and be delivered on time to the intended recipients.

Cost: It should demonstrate that the project has been professionally executed, has been undertaken within the agreed budget and even provided added value.

Quality: The report should be accurate, clear and logically arranged. It should show a depth of investigation consistent with the importance of the subject. It is important that it should only draw conclusions and make recommendations which are aligned with the facts discovered as part of the assignment, in the data collection, the research undertaking or in the practical findings. Introducing new conclusions which do not have this traceability will bring the validity and accuracy of the report into question.

For the report to be well received by the client the above points will need to be addressed. In addition to these is the report writing style of the consultant which will need not only to satisfy the above and the QA requirements but importantly also to be aligned to the preferences of the client audience. This is particularly important if the client intends to pass the consultant's report to other parties.

Presentations

Giving presentations, like report writing and workshop facilitation, should be regarded as second nature for those undertaking a role in management consultancy. However, all these skills need to be learnt and practised if the consultant is to portray a confident ability to undertake work for a client and deliver convincing results. The ability to stand up and present at a flip-chart or whiteboard is deemed to be part of the facilitation skills; the term "presentation" here usually, if not exclusively, refers to slide presentations, produced in MS PowerPoint. In summary, the consultant's role in a presentation is divided into two parts; the first and always the longer part is concerned with the preparation of the subject material; the second part covers the actual delivery in front of the target audience. Whilst the preference of style may need to meet with the consultant's organizational requirements there are still a few common features which need to be considered as part of the preparation as shown in Figure 4.7.

Having prepared the material, and checked it for spelling, flow, logistical issues and how the key messages are conveyed, the consultant's attention can now move to the issues around the actual event. Some of these points may not be within the control of the presenter such as the venue and seating style; however, on occasions there may be an opportunity to influence both of these and some knowledge of audience numbers, their expected level of involvement and their knowledge of the topic may suggest an appropriate room layout. The overall timing of the presentation, especially if part of a series of presentations, will need to be considered; in particular, the expected duration of the audience's required level of concentration. This time should be punctuated with breaks at suitable times, and/or some audience participation if appropriate to the venue and topic.

It is recommended to avoid leaving too large a gap between the presenter and the front row of the audience, and whilst it may be proposed that time for questions has

Presentation criteria	Consultant/presenter to consider . . .
Message	. . . the purpose of the slide and what message it is saying.
Content	. . . is this presented in the best way; is there too much detail which may overwhelm the audience and can this be kept to main bullet points that the consultant can expand upon later. The consultant should use the slide as part of a presentation and as such can supplement what is in the slide in more detail as appropriate. In delivery, it will not be necessary to expand on every bullet point.
Clarity	. . . if the slides present in a clear way. Where the model or slide is complex it is often better to have a sequence of slides which builds this up in logical steps.
Visual impact	. . . do the slides look too crowded and if so can they be divided into a number of additional slides. Can some colour be introduced to relieve the monotony of a single colour text against a uniform background. Highlight the key words or messages in a different colour. The notion that a picture is often "worth a thousand words" applies here but only if the picture is relevant to the message of the presentation and the particular slide.
Timing	. . . are there enough slides to keep the presentation flowing without holding one slide for an overly long time as this becomes a distraction and the attention of the audience is often lost through this reason.
Explanation	. . . do the slides support the theme of the presentation and are they explained. A slide which is not obviously linked to the presentation will leave the audience puzzled before they are free to start listening again.
Length	. . . is the number of slides and more importantly the pace at which they need to be screened appropriate for the audience. Whilst too few slides will be boring and may convey to the client a lack of preparation, too many will prompt comments about "death by PowerPoint".

Figure 4.7 Guidelines for slide presentations.

been planned for the end of the presentation, it can also be a good way to connect with the audience at the start by saying that any important questions will be taken during the presentation, if this would be helpful. The next issue for presenters to consider is when to give the audience any handout materials; some attendees will prefer this at the start or even in advance of the day and may use this to follow the presentation and make additional notes at appropriate times. On the other hand, some will just skip through handouts on the day but at a much faster pace than the presenter's rate of delivery. It can be very distracting to the presenter to see the audience fast page turning as they are speaking and also inhibits audience interaction because they are reading what the consultant wants to say before being covered by the slides.

Prior to the presentation, the venue should be seen and the technology checked to see that it works to the presenter's satisfaction. It is further recommended to have two copies of the presentation available – perhaps one on a laptop and a second on a memory stick so that in the event of some technical problem there still may be an alternative which can be used. Dress code, body language, voice volume or microphone usage should all be seen as important areas which will have to be properly addressed. For some consultants a number of practise presentations will be necessary; for others this may be less so. Where the presentation is part of a number given by the same consultancy company it is important that the style, font, layout, use of bullet points, graphics and so on are the same on all of the presentations as this consistency will convey to the audience and client that this has been considered from a wider perspective and demonstrates a professional approach as part of a consultancy team activity. The alternative of each consultant using their own style can lead to a lack of connectedness or fragmented delivery or negative value perception which inevitably prompts the absolutely opposite conclusion.

The final point to mention is that it is natural for presenters to feel nervous about facing an audience and for even well-experienced presenters to feel some "butterflies in their stomachs". Practise, preparation, control over breathing, knowledge of the subject material and so on can help to reduce such nerves and allow the presenter to control their "butterflies" and at the least allow them to "fly in formation!"

CHAPTER 5

TOP-TEN CONSULTANCY TOOLS

INTRODUCTION

The purpose of this final chapter is to present 10 essential consultancy tools which can be used to provide maximum benefit to the client, and at the same time, form part of a management consultant's natural toolkit. Of course, in practice rarely will all the tools need to be used but a number are interlinked providing a logical progression through the stages of many consultancy interventions and assignments. These tools have been well tested over a period of time; in a range of private and public sector businesses; in organizations small and large; and in many countries across the world.

The ten tools selected allow transition between the high level strategy and operation business issues to be understood and used in a productive way. Furthermore, in the right combination they can be used to present a composite view of an organization's business topography and future landscape. Whilst there will be a number of consultancy situations where these may be used, a description of each together with a typical example of its use and attributes is provided for each model.

TOP-TEN CONSULTANCY TOOLS

1. A Model for Strategic Analysis

This is a widely known and tried, tested and actively used model produced by Professor Michael Porter of Harvard University, and is sometimes referred to as Porter's five forces. It provides a framework to allow an easy analysis of a company, or even industry sector, to be examined. The basic forces of new entrants, substitutes, rivalry, suppliers and buyers are shown in Figure 5.1 and in their expanded form in Figure 5.2 where the text in each of the five forces should prompt the consultant to consider these aspects in relation to the client organization.

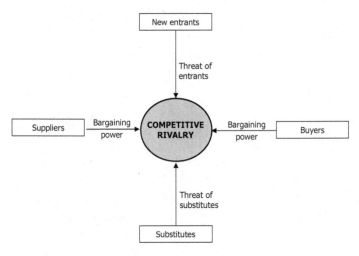

Figure 5.1 Porter's five forces – overview.

Professor Porter's model can be used as part of the organization's strategy planning process and also to ensure that the actions (current or proposed) are aligned with its strategy and its market position aspirations. The use of the detailed model can help to identify where additional information may be required to assist the company in its strategy development with suggestions for future competitive strategies. See also Figure 5.2.

2. SWOT Analysis

Almost every book on management strategy uses the SWOT analysis tool (Figure 5.3) for establishing the

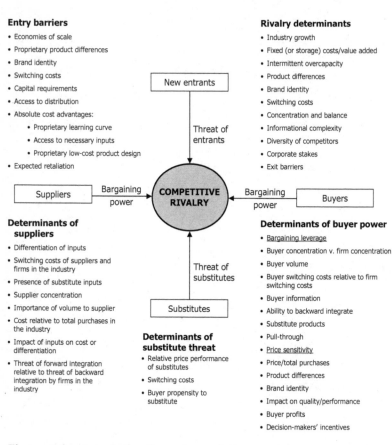

Entry barriers

- Economies of scale
- Proprietary product differences
- Brand identity
- Switching costs
- Capital requirements
- Access to distribution
- Absolute cost advantages:
    - Proprietary learning curve
    - Access to necessary inputs
    - Proprietary low-cost product design
- Expected retaliation

Rivalry determinants

- Industry growth
- Fixed (or storage) costs/value added
- Intermittent overcapacity
- Product differences
- Brand identity
- Switching costs
- Concentration and balance
- Informational complexity
- Diversity of competitors
- Corporate stakes
- Exit barriers

New entrants

Threat of entrants

Suppliers — Bargaining power → **COMPETITIVE RIVALRY** ← Bargaining power — Buyers

Determinants of suppliers

- Differentiation of inputs
- Switching costs of suppliers and firms in the industry
- Presence of substitute inputs
- Supplier concentration
- Importance of volume to supplier
- Cost relative to total purchases in the industry
- Impact of inputs on cost or differentiation
- Threat of forward integration relative to threat of backward integration by firms in the industry

Threat of substitutes

Substitutes

Determinants of substitute threat

- Relative price performance of substitutes
- Switching costs
- Buyer propensity to substitute

Determinants of buyer power

- Bargaining leverage
- Buyer concentration v. firm concentration
- Buyer volume
- Buyer switching costs relative to firm switching costs
- Buyer information
- Ability to backward integrate
- Substitute products
- Pull-through
- Price sensitivity
- Price/total purchases
- Product differences
- Brand identity
- Impact on quality/performance
- Buyer profits
- Decision-makers' incentives

Figure 5.2   Porter's five forces (expanded).

Reprinted with the permission of The Free Press, a Division of Simon & Schuster Adult Publishing Group, from *Competitive Advantage: Creating and Sustaining Superior Performance* by Professor Michael E. Porter. Copyright © 1985, 1998 Michael E. Porter. All rights reserved.

company's strengths, weaknesses, opportunities and the threats, and analysing the output as part of performance improvement processes or in strategy formulation. This tool is particularly helpful for generating a summary of a strategic situation and is applicable to any size of company – from the sole trader to the multi-national organization. Strengths and weaknesses cover the internal attributes of the company and may include skills, expertise or technological "know-how", particular organizational resources, intellectual capital, competitive capabilities or potential advantages. Opportunities and threats typically arise from a company's external competitive environment. In general:

- Strengths usually cover factors such as product or services quality, lower costs than the competition, effective processes and well-trained staff.
- Weaknesses also tend to be internal to the organization such as relative size compared to the competition, size of operation and amount of experience in particular geographic regions when looking at new markets.
- Opportunities are usually derived from factors outside of the organization such as new export market opportunities, difficulties that competitors face, etc.
- Threats are also external in nature and often take the form of competitor actions such as launch of new products rendering the company's goods obsolete or unfashionable.

	Strengths	Weaknesses
Internal to Organization		
External to Organization	Opportunities	Threats

Potential Internal Strengths

- Leading manufacturing capability - plant and equipment
- Good customer relationships with repeat sales
- Long-term contracts
- Skills and knowledge in key areas
- Strong financial results and retained profits
- Recognized as the market leader
- Integrated strategies throughout organization
- Leverage from economies of scale
- Proprietary and patented technology
- Low cost/efficient operations
- Recognized brands through advertising campaigns
- Effective marketing approach and good sales team
- Experienced long-term management teams
- Encouragement of innovation
- Superior products through R&D investment

Potential Internal Weaknesses

- Limited R&D work - trend is to follow rather than lead product design
- Limited or outdated product range. Obsolete facilities and processes
- Limited managerial skills and experience
- Undefined or communicated strategic direction
- Strategy implementation poorly executed or implemented
- Low profit margins or low profitability compared to competitors
- Market reputation poor
- Distribution and logistics network underdeveloped
- Marketing skills below those of competitors
- Absence of key skills or competencies
- Operating problems with plant and equipment

Potential External Opportunities

- Potential to embrace new technologies
- Good prospects for further market development
- Potential to expand into new markets or segments
- Ability to transfer skills and technological know-how to new products or business
- Product line has extension capacity to expand to meet changing customer needs
- Availability of new markets through removal of trade barriers in attractive foreign markets
- Forward and backward integration through supply chain management
- Growth potential due to increased market demand

Potential External Threats

- Foreign competition aided by lower cost of entry to market
- Foreign exchange rates and trade policies of foreign governments affecting overseas markets and value of income
- Changes in demographics consequential impact on product demand
- Increase in sales of substitute products
- Slower market growth than production requirement
- Threat of market recession
- Failure to deliver new products and/or poor product reliability
- Increasing bargaining power of distributors, wholesalers and retailers prior to selling to customers
- Buyer more aware of competitors' products and match to their needs/tastes

Figure 5.3 SWOT matrix.

The SWOT tool can be used by individuals or as a group exercise where it can be used to identify areas for discussion; however, the simplicity of the tool can be a trap and care needs to be taken in using this for two main reasons:

- First, it should not be assumed that completing each quadrant is the full analysis – whilst an organization may have 10 strengths and only two weaknesses it is not the volume of each category but their severity. Indeed, two major weaknesses may easily outweigh 10 strengths based on their weighted impact on the business.

- Second, the factors used to populate the matrix must be regarded as a "snap-shot" at a particular moment in time and as the world changes new opportunities and threats emerge. Furthermore, what are thought to be internal strengths today may not be the same tomorrow.

The output of the SWOT analysis is to examine the internal and external pressures on the business. It has wide use in strategic management, people development, marketing, change management and business planning as it provides a clear indication of where a business is performing well and the areas it needs to address to improve. It can be used as part of a change programme to convert threats into opportunities and internal weaknesses into competitive strengths. As mentioned at the outset this tool has strong linkages with other tools such as those shown in Figures 5.4 and 5.5. The details of a typical SWOT analysis are provided below – this may act as a checklist and aid this process. However, a word of caution in using "checklists" is that they can make the user lazy and may miss SWOT features simply because they are not on the checklist, from which the analysis starts: as such, the advice here is that "the brain still needs to be engaged".

SWOT checklist – a tool to start the process ...

Potential internal strengths

- Leading manufacturing capability – plant and equipment.
- Good customer relationships with repeat sales.
- Long-term contracts.
- Skills and knowledge in key areas.
- Strong financial results and retained profits.
- Recognized as the market leader.
- Integrated strategies throughout organization.
- Leverage from economies of scale.
- Proprietary and patented technology.
- Low cost/efficient operations.
- Recognized brands through advertising campaigns.
- Effective marketing approach and good sales team.
- Experienced long-term management teams.
- Encouragement of innovation.
- Superior products through research and development (R&D) investment.

Potential internal weaknesses

- Limited research and development work – the trend is to follow others rather than lead product design.
- Limited or outdated product range, obsolete facilities and processes.
- Limited managerial skills and experience.
- Undefined or communicated strategic direction.
- Strategy implementation poorly executed or implemented.
- Low profit margins or low profitability compared to competitors.
- Market reputation poor.
- Distribution and logistics network underdeveloped.
- Marketing skills below those of competitors.
- Absence of key skills or competencies.
- Operating problems with plant and equipment.

Potential external opportunities

- Potential to embrace new technologies.
- Good prospects for further market development.
- Potential to expand into new markets or segments.
- Ability to transfer skills and technological know-how to new products or business.
- Product line has extension capacity to expand to meet changing customer needs.
- Availability of new markets through removal of trade barriers in attractive foreign markets.

- Forward and backward integration through supply chain management.
- Growth potential due to increased market demand.

Potential external threats

- Foreign competition aided by lower cost of entry to market.
- Foreign exchange rates and trade policies of foreign governments affecting overseas markets and value of income.
- Changes in demographics and consequential impact on product demand.
- Increase in sales of substitute products.
- Slower market growth than production requirement.
- Threat of market recession.
- Failure to deliver new products and/or poor product reliability.
- Increasing bargaining power of distributors, wholesalers and retailers prior to selling to customers.
- Buyer more aware of competitors' products and match to their needs/tastes.

3. Strategic Formulation Process

This model provides an approach though a framework within which a business strategy can be developed and implemented. It can be seen that the SWOT analysis is

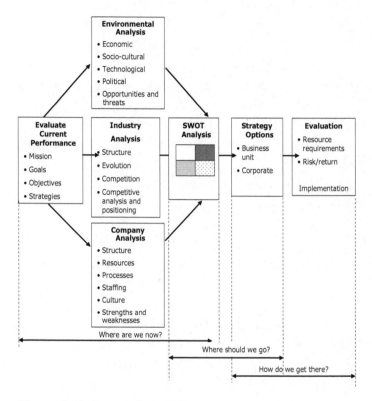

Figure 5.4 Strategy formulation.
From Cornelis A. de Kluyver and John A. Pearce, *Strategy: A View from the Top*, 1st edition, 2003. Electronically reproduced by permission of Pearson Education Inc., Upper Saddle River, New Jersey, USA.

featured here and the main theme is in understanding where the company is at present, its future desired direction and how this objective may be achieved. The area entitled "Environmental Analysis" comprises the PEST

(Political, Economic, Social, Technology) technique or expanded PESTLE (with the addition of Legal and Environmental) which can also be used to identify and address external issues which are likely to act on product/services launch and operations. In today's business climate this is often a useful tool in exploring the external business factors and how the organization needs to respond to, or capitalize on, this information.

This structure addresses other management areas including business planning and market research.

4. Understanding the Product/Services

This is a useful tool which the consultant can use to better understand a product or service business within a client organization and can then use to link this understanding to the previous SWOT analysis. The questions can be combined together with envisioning the future for the organization and identifying associated barriers or constraints and can also assist in promoting the planning process. It can be linked into a workshop format to maximize on the amount of stakeholder involvement, creative thinking and client agreement in developing a way forward.

This model forms part of the strategic planning process and has applicability which can be related to corporate, business unit or work group levels and seeks alignment with the strategic direction of the organiza-

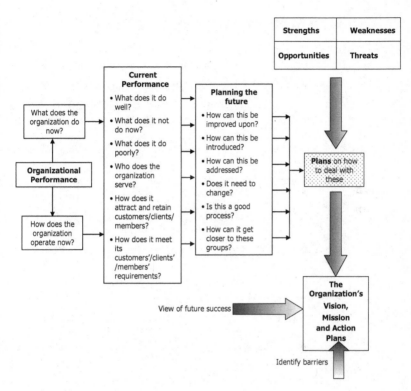

Figure 5.5 Understanding the product/service.
Adapted from *The Essential Management Toolbox: Tools, Models and Notes for Managers and Consultants*, S.A. Burtonshaw-Gunn, 2008.

tion's vision and mission statements. The prompt questions below can then be related to an organization's marketing activities, see also Figures 5.6, 5.7 and 5.10 and in addressing these the relationship with the models in Figures 5.8 and 5.9 may also be beneficial.

5. The Marketing Mix

The traditional elements of marketing – often referred to as the "Marketing Mix" or the "4Ps" – are shown below. Additional inputs developed by Bernard Booms and Mary

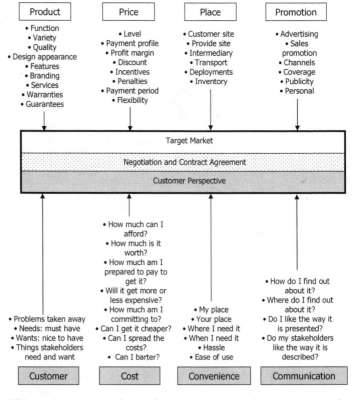

Figure 5.6 Using the marketing mix to match customer needs. From *The Essential Management Toolbox: Tools, Models and Notes for Managers and Consultants*, S.A. Burtonshaw-Gunn, 2008.

Bitner in 1981 after Professor Kotler's original Marketing Mix model are discussed in detail in *Essential Tools for Marketing*. The elements can be used to assist management decisions on the product/service in relation to the marketplace. With respect to the original 4Ps, the 'Price' needs to be considered in relation to what the market can stand; the 'Product' (or services) that the organization offers needs to be detailed including features and benefits with the most significant likely to include function, appearance and status. In looking at 'Promotion' this will have to address the options for how the customers will know and differentiate the product or services. Finally, 'Place' refers to the contact points where the product or service will be sold. All of these elements will need to be addressed in the marketing plan.

The 4Ps can be used match the identified customer needs ideally gained from undertaking market research, customer focus groups, complaints, etc.

6. Product Performance Analysis

The Boston Consultancy Group's Growth/Share matrix approach to portfolio analysis in based on observations in the 1970s that multi-divisional, multi-product companies have a strong advantage over non-diversified companies: the ability to channel resources into the most productive units. This matrix has remained widely used since this time to examine the relative market share and the market growth rate. Using the BCG matrix provides knowledge

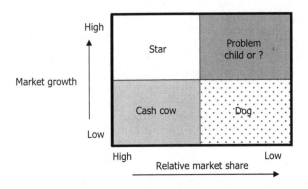

Figure 5.7   Product performance matrix.
The BCG Product Portfolio Matrix reproduced with kind permission of the Boston Consulting Group Inc. © Copyright 1970. All rights reserved.

on which to undertake decision making as part of the strategic planning process and to gain agreement on the general direction of the marketing strategy.

Within the four categories:

- **Stars** are usually products with high cash generation, but are likely to require further investment.
- **Problem child** or **Question mark** is usually newly launched products or ones in difficulty, such as low market share in a growing market; these generate low cash and require high cash injection.
- **Cash cow** is usually a product which generates high cash flow from a dominant market position in a declining or static market. This is likely to require careful maintenance but low cash input.

- **Dogs** are products which have
  little or limited market sector
  of cash generation. The demand
  likely to be in decline.

An organization's products can be plotted aga.
two axis of the matrix with respect to differential grow.
rates and diversified markets. A further refinement can
be made by plotting on this matrix circles whose scale
can represent the contribution that each product has to
the organization. Based on this new information the following actions may then be taken:

- **Stars:** Invest to improve competitive position in an
  attractive market.
- **Question mark:** Exit – divest in a weak competitive position.
- **Cash cow:** Maintain and protect in a competitive
  position.
- **Dogs:** Harvest, relinquish any competitive position
  in favour of a short-term profit and cash flow now
  or alternatively exit/divest altogether.

7. The Change Pyramid

Recognition of the need to justify, communicate and
train staff in change management to minimize resistance
to proposed change not only needs to be sensitively
managed, but has always been a feature of undertaking
change from established practices across the ages. The

vice penned by the sixteenth century Italian courtier
Nicholo Machiavelli is often quoted by those involved
in undertaking this task:

> There is nothing more difficult to take in hand, more peril-
> ous to conduct, or more uncertain in its success, than to
> take the lead in the introduction of a new order of things.
> **(From *The Prince* published in 1532)**

Bearing in mind the above historical advice and the
recognition of the level of difficulty of introducing change,
the model shown as Figure 5.8 shows there is a range of
changes which an organization may wish to realize. The
model proposes that the easier changes at the bottom of
the pyramid offer the least level of discomfort for employ-

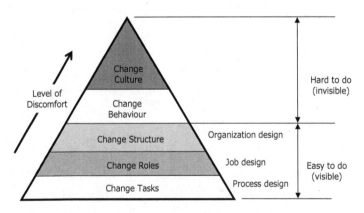

Figure 5.8   The change pyramid.
From *The Essential Management Toolbox: Tools, Models and Notes
for Managers and Consultants*, S.A. Burtonshaw-Gunn, 2008.

ees and hence require less time and cost to implement. Similarly, the higher levels necessitate substantial time and investment and are much harder to implement. The pyramid model also suggests that embarking on the lower level changes first may be a good way to develop an acceptance to a change programme especially if quick, beneficial and easy to observe results can be realized by this staged approach – a clear example of harvesting "the low hanging fruit" first or "quick wins" key to demonstrating credibility for client organization buy-in.

For those contemplating the highest level of organizational change there are a few examples of how this has been undertaken; in the main this is perhaps because of the level of investment in time, money and other resources that large-scale cultural change demands. However, among the international companies achieving success in this area was British Aerospace in the mid-1990s, although even after considerable investment across its business footprint involving all staff and indeed engagement and participation with its customers much of this was diluted with the formation of BAE Systems by BAE and Marconi Systems in 1999. Nevertheless, the details of the cultural transformation programme are documented in the then chairman's account in the publication "Vertical Take-off" where the focus of the changes was centred on the organization's core values of Partnership, People, Performance, Customer, Innovation and Technology with each being championed throughout the organization by local, regional and board level managers.

8. Change Strategies

Before considering change – what type of change, how to do it, identifying who is to be involved or who is affected by any change programme, two points need to be made. First, it is absolutely crucial to gain the most senior level support and commitment as any change management plan is destined to fail unless supported by a main sponsor, often the senior management of the organization, the organization's stakeholders and in some cases its customer base too. Second, acceptance is needed within the organization that such recommended change is seen as being appropriate for the specific business. On this basis acceptance by the management of the business plan objective and its change recommendations will then allow them to consider the type of change strategy best suited to pursue a new direction or initiate changes necessary to facilitate increased organizational performance.

There are a number of factors that will need to be considered by the management in choosing how to implement the necessary changes, as each approach will be appropriate in different circumstances. Indeed, those that are inconsistent with the demands of the situation – the people, the cultural setting and the business environment – will undoubtedly run into problems and fail to support and embed the long-term required changes.

In agreeing an appropriate strategy or combination of strategies for change, the organization's management will need to take into account the following factors:

Figure 5.9 Change strategies.
From *Change Management and Organizational Performance* by Professor Simon A. Burtonshaw-Gunn and Dr Malik G. Salameh, 2007. Reproduced with permission of ICFAI University Press, Hyderabad, India.

- The degree of opposition expected.
- The power base of the change initiator.
- The need for information, communication and commitment when planning and carrying out the change.
- The nature of the current organization's culture and its likely response to change.

After considering the above factors there are five broad optional approaches which can be deployed in change implementation. The consultant should be well placed to discuss these with the client as part of the scoping and selecting the most appropriate strategy for the client organization and consultancy assignment.

Directive Strategy

A directive strategy allows the management to use its authority to impose the business changes required and will be able to carry them out speedily. However, the disadvantage of this approach is that it is likely to increase resistance or even undermine change implementation.

Expert Strategy

This approach is usually applied when a "technical" problem requires solving, such as, for example, the introduction of a new IT system. It is a sensible strategy to adopt when only a limited number of employees have the technical knowledge to comment on the changes proposed, other than in general terms.

Negotiating Strategy

This strategy involves a willingness to negotiate with individuals and teams affected by the change and to accept that adjustments and concessions may have to be made. Opting for this approach does not remove the management's responsibility for the direction and initiation of change, but acknowledges that those affected have the right to have some input in the changes proposed, or that they have some power to resist it if they are not supportive. The advantage of this approach is that resistance to change is likely to be less; however, the implementation time may take longer as consensus is sought. Changing work practices in return for increased pay and/or other benefits is a classic example of the negotiating strategy.

Educative Strategy

The educative strategy involves changing people's values and beliefs so that they support the change and are committed to a shared set of organizational values. Winning "hearts and minds" is a complex process that involves a mixture of activities, such as communication, persuasion, education, training and selection.

The advantage of such an approach, if successful, is that people will be positively committed to the change. In general this approach typically takes much longer and requires more resources than the previous three strategies.

Participative Strategy

This last option offers the client organization a number of advantages: changes are more likely to be widely acceptable over the others; it promotes the active involvement of people; and is likely to increase their commitment to and enthusiasm for the change process. Additionally, there will be opportunities for both managers and employees to learn from the experiences and skills of this wide participation.

Whilst this has a number of advantages due to the participation of staff, the identified changes are likely to take longer and require additional resources to support the change.

The topic of change management features as a full chapter in *Essential Tools for Organizational Performance*, covering approaches to change management, programming, the people issues around implementing change and in dealing with any resistance to proposed changes.

9. Check on Business Plan Feasibility

This is a very useful tool to examine and test the integrity of an organization's business plan, which is likely be derived as a result of the strategic analysis, SWOT, marketing and market/product analysis seen in the other models in this chapter. It is suggested that success in business depends on the following three crucial elements; namely, the management of the business, its approach to marketing and the amount of money that the business needs and will generate. Each of these three elements are detailed below which may be used by the consultant to test the proposed business plan and provide the client's organization with a level of confidence before it presents its business plan to external investors or stakeholders.

Example business plans and their production are described further in the *Essential Tools for Operations Management*.

Management	Does the management team have the motivation and skills to deliver the products/services you envisage?
	Does the management team have the skills to look after the administration side of the business, including all of the money matters?
	Has the organization the ability to sell the services to the potential clients identified?
	Are you prepared to modify the business plan in the light of what people want?
	Is the company confident that it is able to manage skills and time to full effect?
	Does it need any new people to make this plan work?
	Does it need "different" people to make the plan work?
	Can the plan work and the business carry on if current key people leave the company for another job, retire, win the lottery, etc.?
Marketing	What is so special about the services that the company intends to provide?
	How do you know that anyone will want to buy them?
	How often will they buy from you?
	How much will you charge for the services and are people/companies prepared to pay those prices?
	Are you sure that you can provide these services at these prices, make a profit and manage the cash flow?
	Why should anyone buy from the company rather than others in the market?
	Is this the right time to start providing the services that you have in mind?
	Will you be able to develop them as the market develops?
	Have you considered how you will advertise or promote the company's services and how much will this cost? (See also "Money" below.)
	Where will you advertise or promote?
	Do you know who the competitors are and what services/products they are selling?
	Have you spoken to any potential customers about the company's services that you provide or intend to provide?
Money	Will the business make a profit?
	Will you be able to pay each bill as it arrives?
	What financial resources will you need to be successful?
	Are you confident that you can pay back any loans over a reasonable period, and pay the interest?
	Have you researched, listed and costed the expenditure items that you will incur?
	When will income start to flow?
	Which part of the market provides the revenue? Is this secure or high risk?
	What are customers prepared to pay for the company's services?
	What revenue can we expect from new markets?
	What revenue can we get from repeat business?
	What is the cost of acquiring new business, in bidding, making contacts, marketing, presentations, etc.?

Figure 5.10 Business plan feasibility check.
From *The Essential Management Toolbox: Tools, Models and Notes for Managers and Consultants*, S.A. Burtonshaw-Gunn, 2008.

10. Continued Performance

Having perhaps undertaken an analysis of the business, identified changes and improvements and implemented a change management programme, it will be crucial that such investment is not regarded only as a short-term benefit. On completion of a major change the business focus should move to one of continual, incremental improvement. The final tool selected provides a series of key questions around the "Six honest men" from Rudyard Kipling's poem which serves as a framework for examining approaches to improvement by questioning current or proposed operations. In practice this tool can be used by consultants as the basis for individual investigation of problems; as a framework for interviews; and as an enabling tool within a facilitated performance management workshop environment.

Continuous improvement is also discussed as part of process management and business process re-engineering within *Essential Tools for Organizational Performance*. This also provides other useful tools to support continuous performance following a process mapping activity.

Text of the "Six honest men" by Rudyard Kipling, from "The Elephant's Child" in the *Just So Stories* published in 1904

Figure 5.11 An approach to continuous improvement.
From *The Essential Management Toolbox: Tools, Models and Notes for Managers and Consultants*, S.A. Burtonshaw-Gunn, 2008. Text of the "Six honest men" by Rudyard Kipling from "The Elephant's Child" in the *Just So Stories*, published in 1904.

REFERENCES

Burtonshaw-Gunn, S.A. (2005) Extending the concept of "Added-Value" to Consultancy, *Professional Consultancy Magazine*, Issue 14. Institute of Management Consultants, UK.

Burtonshaw-Gunn, S.A. (2007) Networking – a personal view, *Professional Consultancy Magazine*, Issue 20. Institute of Management Consultants, UK.

Burtonshaw-Gunn, S.A. and Salameh, M.G. (2007) *Change Management and Organizational Performance*. ICAFI University Press, Hyderabad, India. June 2007.

Burtonshaw-Gunn, S.A. (2008) *Essential Management Toolbox: Models, Tools and Notes for Managers and Consultants*. John Wiley and Sons, UK. ISBN 9780470518373.

Burtonshaw-Gunn, S.A. and Salameh, M.G. (2009) *Essential Tools for Organizational Performance*. John Wiley and Sons, UK. ISBN 9780470746653.

Burtonshaw-Gunn, S.A. (2009) *Risk and Financial Management in Construction*. Gower Publishing, UK. ISBN 9780566088971.

Burtonshaw-Gunn, S.A. (2010) *Essential Tools for Operations Management*. John Wiley and Sons, UK. ISBN 9780470745922.

Connor, R. and Davidson, J. (1997) *Marketing Your Consulting and Professional Services*. Published by John Wiley and Sons, UK. ISBN 9780471133926.

de Kluyver, C.A. and Pearce, J.A. (2003) *Strategy: A View from the Top*, 1st edition. Pearson Education Inc., Upper Saddle River, New Jersey. ISBN 9780130083607.

Evans, Sir Richard and Price, C. (2000) *Vertical Take-off*. Nicholas Brealey. ISBN 9781857882452.

Eve, N. *The Facilitator's Development Programme Course Manual*. Elements, UK.

Fox, K. (2004) *Watching the English – The Hidden Rules of English Behaviour*. Hodder and Stoughton Ltd, London. ISBN 9780340818862.

Gladwell, M. (2000) *The Tipping Point*. Little Brown and Company, UK. ISBN 9780316316965.

International Labour Organization (1996) *Management Consulting: A Guide to the Profession*. ILO Geneva, 3rd edition. ISBN 9221094499.

Institute of Business Consulting (2002) *Management Consultancy Competence Framework*.

Jacobs, M. (2000) *Swift to Hear – Facilitating Skills in Listening and Responding*. SPCK Publishing, UK. ISBN 9780281052608.

Kipling, Rudyard. "Six honest men" from "The Elephant's Child" in the *Just So Stories*, first published in 1904.

Leach, J. and Moon, J. (2003) *Pitch Perfect*. Capstone Publishing Limited. ISBN 9781841125817.

Margerison, C.J. (2001) *Managerial Consulting – A Practical Guide*. Gower Publishing, UK, 2nd edition. ISBN 9780566082924.

Porter, M.E. (1985) *Competitive Advantage: Creating and Sustaining Superior Performance*. The Free Press, USA. ISBN 9780029250907.

Raghavan, A. (2006) Ethics and governance – next global frontier for India Inc, from *Business Daily*, The Hindu group of publications, India. July 15, 2006.

Robson, C. (2002) *Real World Research*, 2nd edition. Wiley Blackwell Publishing. ISBN 9780631213055.

Schien, E.F. (1988) *Process Consultation, its Role in Organizational Development*. Addison–Wesley Publishing. ISBN 9780201067366.

Townsend, R. (1970) *Up the Organisation*. Alfred A. Knopf. ISBN 9780394450346.

Weiss, D. (1999) *High Impact HR: Transforming Human Resources for Competitive Advantage*. John Wiley and Sons Canada Limited. ISBN 9780471643852.

Worsley, P. (1992) *The New Introducing Sociology*, 3rd edition. Penguin, London. Contributors: F. Bechhofer, R. Brown, M. Jeffreys, M. Mcintosh, H. Newby, J. Rex, W. Sharrock, J. Young and M. Young. ISBN 9780140135947. First published as *Introducing Sociology*. Penguin Books 1970.

WEBSITES

UK Foreign and Commonwealth Office (FCO)
www.fco.gov.uk

Institute of Business Consulting
www.ibconsulting.org.uk

Facilitator's Development Programme, Elements Limited
www.elementsuk.com

ADDRESSES

Professional Contractors Group Ltd, Heathrow Boulevard, Bath Road, West Drayton UB7 0DQ

Institute of Business Consulting, 4th Floor, 2 Savoy Court Strand, London WC2R 0EZ

Institute of Business Ethics, 24 Greencoat Place, London SW1P 1BE

International Business Ethics Institute, 145–157 St John Street, London EC1V 4PY

INDEX

Index compiled by Annette Musker

Printed and bound by CPI Group (UK) Ltd, Croydon, CR0 4YY